영 어 회 화
요것만 알면!

AMERICAN IDIOMS : Conversation Made Easy

영어회화 요것만 알면!

미국인이 즐겨 쓰는 영어회화
가나다 순으로 찾기 쉬운 585가지

김순관

미지출판

일상 영어회화가 쉬우면서도 어렵다는 사실을 새삼 느끼게 된 것은 1979년 미국 유학 생활을 시작하면서부터였다. 그때는 이미 대학원 과정을 포함하여 12년 동안이나 영어 학습을 마치고 학교에서 15년 넘게 영어를 가르치고 있었던 후였다. 그런데도 원어민(native speaker)과의 대화에서 그들의 말을 잘 알아듣지 못하고 또 필자의 말도 상대방이 이해를 못했으니 얼마나 답답했는지 모른다.

그 원인은 필자의 귀가 그들의 발음에 익숙하지 못한 탓도 있었지만 꼭 그 원인만은 아니었다. 예를 들어 원어민으로부터 "You're pulling my leg?"라는 말을 들었을 때 나는 상대방의 다리를 쳐다보았다. 이와 동시에 상대방의 웃음이 터져 나왔다. 분명 pull도 배우고 leg도 배웠지만 이것이 "나를 놀리는 거니?"라는 뜻으로 쓰인다는 것을 나중에 알았을 때 참으로 쓴웃음을 지을 수밖에 없었다.

한번은 노총각(?) 미국인과 이야기를 하다가 결혼이 늦은 이유를 묻자, 그는 "I'd like to play the field."라고 대답했다. play나 field란 어휘가 사용된 데다가 체격도 좋아서 필자는 아마 그가 예전에 축구선수나 야구선수였나 보다고 추측했다. 나중에 play the field가 결혼은 하지 않고 이 사람 저 사람과 데이트만 하는 것이라는 의미를 알게 되었을 때는 추측이 얼마나 빗나간 것이었는가를 알고 놀랐다.

나처럼 많은 사람들이 미국 사람과의 대화에서 추측으로 대충 이해하고 넘겨버리기 일쑤다. butterfly나 stomach는 중학교 과정에서 기본 단어로 배운다. 그러면 "I have butterflies in my stomach."은 어떤 의미일까?

이런 여러 가지 아쉬움에서 30여 년 전 이 책 초판을 출간하여 13쇄까지 찍었다. 그 후 정말 긴 세월이 흘렀지만 초판에서 미흡했던 부분과 지금 미국인들이 즐겨 쓰는 생활영어를 고르고 보충하여 개정판을 내게 되었으니 본인으로서는 감회가 새로울 따름이다.

이 책은 우리말의 가나다순으로 편집되어 있어 한글에 익숙한 사람이 적당한 때와 장소에 따라 쉽게 활용할 수 있다. 또한 원어민과 대화할 때 꼭 필요한 표현들을 골라 수록했으므로 미국식 영어에 익숙해지는 데 꼭 필요한 책이라고 생각한다.

아무쪼록 이 책이 여러분의 영어회화에 큰 도움이 될 수 있기를 바란다. 또한 이 책이 나올 수 있게 배려해 주신 이지출판사 서용순 대표와 박성현 실장에게 깊이 감사드린다. 그리고 물심양면으로 도움을 준 아내와 아들 인수, 딸 혜련과 혜진에게 고마움을 전한다.

2018년 여름

김 순 관

Editors' Forward

Professor Kim, who is an alumnus of Western Illinois University, is an individual known and respected by all of the editorial board. Many of the expressions he has included in his book are a direct result of conversation with us. Professor Kim has had an insatiable desire to learn and understand American idioms. This desire has translated itself from his own study into this unique book. Because idioms are so culture-based, Professor Kim brought his book to us in the United States for complete evaluation before it was published. Each of us has read a section of the book, revised where necessary, and determined that phrases included are still current in American conversation. To the best of our knowledge, the result is an extensive and current text of American idioms and slang.

Ronald W. Bradley, Former Director
WESL Institute
Western Illinois University

Carleen S. Johnson, Secretary
WESL Institute
Western Illinois University

Mary M. Davern, Former Director
Foreign Student Affairs
Western Illinois University

Patricia I. Jones, Asst. Director
Foreign Student Affairs
Western Illinois University

Lu Pearson Smith, Director
Foreign Student Admissions office
Western Illinois University

While working at Seoul Foreign School and traveling extensively through much of Korea for the last three years my wife and I have encountered many gratifying as well as many frustrating experiences. The gratifying experiences stem largely from the out-going kindness so many Koreans have demonstrated toward us(i. e. flagging down a taxi for us in the rain or actually taking time away from their work to show us the way to a difficult-to-find restroom). The frustrating experiences, as you might guess, stem from the limited communication that we can engage in with these "good Samaritan" Koreans.

Of course we are partly to blame for this frustration, as my ability in speaking Korean is limited to market, travel, and eating phrases(often improper at that!). Yet another part of the blame lies in the way Koreans learn English throughout high school and college–that is the formal textbook approach. The problem with this method is that it teaches English only the way Americans would speak at a public address or respond in print. It basically ignores personal communication. For instance, we would never say in personal conversation that "His English ability has made significant progress this semester." Rather, we would put it this way : "His English has really taken off lately!" The sooner English educators in Korea recognize that Americans generally speak in an informal manner, the sooner Korean-American communication will become more personal and gratifying for both parties ; thus building lasting friendships.

In my estimation Professor Kim, Soon Kwan's AMERICAN IDIOMS : Conversation Made Easy "fits the bill" for all those in Korea who desire to learn conversational English the way Americans speak it at work, at play, and in the home. His study of English idioms while attending my Stateside university some five years ago really impressed me because every time an unfamiliar common expression would come up in our conversation he would faithfully "jot" it down on his alwayshandy notepad and then double-check the meaning of the phrase to "zero-in" on its proper use (*timing and situation are very important in using idiomatic expressions to achieve the desired effect-deeper communication). The author' s knowledge and use of informal English conversation certainly has been a large factor in our staying in Korea this long, as well as coming to a land so far from our comfortable life in the U.S. in the first place.

The book itself, while not being exhaustive, definitely is an extensive survey of often-used expressions in English conversation. The "Hangul" alphabetization will serve as a time saving guide to the time conscious Korean. Another timesaving help is the index, illustrating both page numbers and phrase (*note that each of some 1,050 idioms is used in meaningful English phrases) numbers.

Because of the aforementioned reasons I strongly endorse this book for middle and high school English teachers, English conversation instructors at both the institute and university levels, those engaged in any realm of international business (including those who work in the industry of Korean tourism), and really anyone who has a general interest in learning more practical English.

One last thing for those who hope or plan to study abroad in the United States (as this seems to be a growing trend among Koreans) : this book is a MUST if you intend to minimize the oncoming culture shock and alienation from your American peers. To maximize your understanding and hopefully avoid some of the frustration my wife and I have experienced while living in Korea, you must learn the type of English conversation that will promote personal friendships ; and thus make your U.S. stay a truly gratifying one. AMERICAN IDIOMS : Conversation Made Easy is a major step in that direction

Brian L. Galloway

High School History Teacher

Seoul Foreign School

CONTENTS

마

바

사

아

자

차

가

001 가능성이 반반이다

a fifty-fifty chance

DIALOG 1

A : 가능성이 어떻다고 생각해요?

What do you think your chances are?

B : **반반이라고** 생각해요.

I think **fifty-fifty**.

DIALOG 2

A : 복권에 당첨될 승산이 있나요?

Are you sure you'll win the lottery?

B : **가능성은 반반입니다.**

There's a fifty-fifty chance.

002 가능성이 희박하다

Chances are slim.

DIALOG

A : 직장을 구할 수 있는 것이 확실한가요?

Are you sure you can land a job?

B : 그렇게 생각지 않아요. **가능성이 희박해요.**

I don't think so. **Chances are slim.**

[Note] land 얻다, 차지하다, 획득하다(secure, obtain)

003 가물에 콩 나듯 하다
once in a blue moon

DIALOG

A : 그를 자주 방문하나요?

Do you visit him often?

B : 아니요, **아주 가끔** 방문해요(**가물에 콩 나듯 합니다**).

No, I visit him **once in a blue moon**.

[Note] once in a blue moon 아주 드물게, 거의 없게(seldom, almost never)

004 가지고 가실 건가요? 여기서 드실 건가요?
Here or to go?

DIALOG

A : 부인, 무엇을 드시겠어요?

What would you like, madam?

B : 콜라 두 잔과 커피 두 잔 주세요.

I'd like two cokes and two coffees, please.

A : **여기서 드실 건가요, 가지고 가실 건가요**?

Here or to go?

B : **가지고 갈 수 있게** 해 주세요.

Make them **to go**, please.

005 각자 부담하다
go Dutch

DIALOG

A : 식사에 모시고 싶습니다.

I'd like to take you out to dinner.

B : 저도 가고 싶긴 합니다만 **각자 부담하기로** 해요.

I'd like to go, but I insist we **go Dutch**.

006 감기 기운이 있다

I'm coming down with a cold.

DIALOG

A : 창백해 보이는데 아프세요?

You look pale. Are you sick?

B : **감기 기운이 있는데** 더 심해지지 않도록 해야겠어요.

I think **I'm coming down with a cold** and I'd like to keep it from getting worse.

A : 조심하시는 것이 좋아요. 감기가 많이 유행하고 있어요.

You'd better take care. There're a lot of colds going around.

[Note] come down with~ (병의) ~기운이 있다(become sick with)/keep (prevent) A from ~ing A가 ~하는 것을 막다/get worse 악화되다, 더 심해지다.

007 거저나 마찬가지다

That's a steal.

DIALOG

A : 그 드레스는 얼마예요?

How much will the dress cost?

B : 20불이에요.

Only $20.

A : 20불이라니 **거저나 마찬가지군요.**

That's a steal at $20.

[Note] steal 값이 굉장히 싼 물건/This dress is a steal at $20.

008 건강이 나쁘다
be out of shape

DIALOG

A : 저는 **건강이** 정말 **나빠요.**

I'm really **out of shape.**

B : 체육관에서 운동을 할 필요가 있군요.

You need to work out at the gym.

[Note] work out 운동하다

009 건강을 유지하다
keep in shape

DIALOG

A : 건강이 좋아 보이는군요.

You're looking good.

B : 고마워요. 저는 **건강을 유지하려고** 노력하고 있어요.

Thanks. I try to **keep in shape.**

(혹은 I try to **stay in good condition.**)

010 (당신의 승진을 위해) 건배합시다
Let's toast your promotion.

DIALOG 1

A : 당신의 승진을 위해 **건배합시다.**

Let's toast your promotion.

B : 고마워요. 정말 친절하시군요.

Thanks. You're very nice.

[Note] A : 자, 우리 우정을 위해 건배합시다.

Here's to our friendship.

B : 건배!

Cheers!

C : 우리 사업의 첫 해를 위해 건배합시다.

I propose a toast to our first year in business.

011 겁이 나서 죽겠다(겁에 질리다)
I'm scared to death.

DIALOG

A : 다음 차례는 너야.

You're on next.

B : 알아요. **겁이 나서 죽겠어요.**

I know. **I'm scared to death.**

A : 그렇게 초조해하지 마. 잘 해낼 거야.

Don't be nervous. You'll do fine.

[Note] 자네는 아무것도 겁낼 것이 없네. You have nothing to be afraid of.

012 결근하겠다고 전화하다
call in sick

DIALOG

A : 닥터 김이 아파서 **결근하겠다고 전화가 왔어요.** 그분은 전부터 아파왔어요.

Dr. Kim **called in sick.** He's really been feeling under the weather.

B : 아마 의사한테 가 봐야 될 거야.

Maybe he needs to see a doctor.

[Note] be (feel) under the weather 몸이 편치 않다.

013 결정하지(짓지) 못하고 있다
Everything's up in the air.

DIALOG

A : 저는 선생님께서 이번 주에 미국에 가시는 줄로 생각했습니다.
I thought you were going to the States this week.

B : 계획이 바뀌었어요. **모든 것을 결정하지 못하고 있어요.**
The plans have been changed. **Everything's up in the air.**

[Note] be up in the air 결정하지 않은, 미정의/Our plans for a vacation are still up in the air. 방학에 대한 계획은 아직 미정이에요.

014 계획대로 잘 되어 가다
Everything's going pretty well on schedule.

DIALOG

A : 작업이 어떻게 되어 가고 있나요?
How's your work coming along?

B : 모든 것이 **계획대로** 잘 되어 가고 있어요.
Everything's going pretty well **on schedule.**

015 까다롭게 고르다
You're too choosy.

DIALOG 1

A : 어느 넥타이를 사야 할지 결정을 내리지 못하겠어요.
I can't decide which necktie to buy.

B : **너무 까다롭게 고르시는군요.** 다 좋은데요.

You're too choosy. They're all nice.

A : 그래요, 하지만 아주 멋졌으면 좋겠어요.

Yes, but it has to be perfect.

[Note] choos(e)y 이것저것 가리는, 까다로운(particular in choosing)

016 고장나다

It's on the blink.

DIALOG

A : 찌꺼기 처리기가 또 **고장이에요.**

The garbage disposal is **on the blink** again.

B : 당장 고쳐야겠어요.

We have to get that thing fixed right away.

[Note] on the blink 고장이 난(out of order)/Our refrigerator went on the blink and much of our food was spoiled. 우리 냉장고가 고장이 나서 음식이 많이 상했어요.

017 고약한

really mean

DIALOG

A : 나는 그의 거만한 미소가 싫어요.

I don't like that arrogant smile he's wearing.

B : 그가 누군데요?

Who is he?

A : 그는 새로운 사장이에요. **고약한 사람**이지요.

He's my new boss. He's **really mean**.

018 고쳐 매다(입다) (넥타이나 옷 등을)
adjust

DIALOG

A : 넥타이를 **고쳐 매셔야** 되겠어요. 삐뚤어졌어요.
You need to **adjust** your tie. It's crooked.

B : 아무리 **고쳐 매도** 형편없어 보이는군요.
No matter how I **adjust this tie**, it still looks terrible.

019 고학으로 대학을 마치다
work one's way through college

DIALOG

A : 졸업을 축하합니다. **고학으로 대학을 마친다는 것이** 매우 힘든 일임에 틀림없어요.
Congratulations on your graduation. It must have been tough for you to **work your way through college**.

B : 그래요. 그렇지만 해냈어요.
It was, but I managed somehow.

020 골칫덩어리(골칫거리)
a pest(nuisance, pain in the neck)

DIALOG

A : 톰이 아직도 다른 아이들을 괴롭히나요?
Does Tom still keep bothering other children?

B : 네, 그 애는 선생님의 **골칫덩어리입니다.**
Yes, he's the teacher's **pest(nuisance)**.

A : 잭은 어때요?
What about Jack?

B : 오, 그 아이는 선생님의 총애를 받고 있어요. 공부를 가장 열심히 하는 학생이지요.

Oh, he's the teacher's pet. He's the most studious pupil.

[Note] pet 특별히 귀여워하는 동물, 애완동물, 귀염둥이(favorite), 소중한 사람(물건)

A : 빌리는 학급에서 착실한 아인가요?

Is Billy a good boy in class?

B : 아뇨. 그 애도 선생님에게 성가신 존재이지요.

No. He is another pain in the neck for the teacher.

021 곰곰이 생각하다
sleep on something

DIALOG

A : 저의 제안을 **곰곰이 생각해 보시고** 내일 아침에 대답해 주세요.

Just **sleep on my offer** and give me your answer tomorrow morning.

B : 그건 전혀 불가능합니다.

It's absolutely out of the question.

022 공간을 차지하다
take up much room(space)

DIALOG

A : 어디에서 야채를 기르나요?

Where do you grow vegetables?

B : 뒷뜰에요. **많은 공간을 차지하지 않아요.**

In my backyard. **They don't take up much room(space).**

023 공상에 잠기다(공중 누각을 짓다)
daydream, build castles in the air

DIALOG

A : 존이 뭘하고 있는 것처럼 보이나요?
What does it look like John's doing?

B : **공상에 잠겨 있는 것** 같군요.
It looks like he's **daydreaming**.

024 공해를 제거하다
get rid of pollution

DIALOG

A : 공해는 발전의 일부분이다.
Pollution is part of progress.

B : **공해를 제거하는 것도** 역시 발전의 일부분이다.
Getting rid of pollution is also part of progress.

025 과반수를 차지하다
make up the majority

DIALOG

A : 너의 반에는 여학생들이 많이 있니?
Are there many co-eds in your class?

B : 네, **과반수를 차지하고 있어요.**
Yes, girls **make up the majority**.

026 괜찮고말고요
by all means

DIALOG 1

A : 미국 달러로 계산을 지불해도 될까요?

May I pay the bill with American dollars?

B : 네, **괜찮고말고요.**

Yes, **by all means.**

DIALOG 2

A : 들어가서 그와 잠깐 이야기해도 될까요?

May I go in and talk with him a moment?

B : **되고말고요.**

By all means.

027 괴롭히다

pick on, bother, bug, annoy

DIALOG

A : 당신이 사장과 사이가 좋지 않다고 들었어요.

I heard you're not getting along too well with your boss.

B : 그 사람이 아무것도 아닌 일로 늘 절 **괴롭혀서** 제 생활을 비참하게 하거든요.

Because he always makes my life miserable, **picking on** me for the slightest thing.

028 교대로 하다

take turns

DIALOG

A : 운전으로 피곤하지 않았어요?

Didn't the driving make you tired?

B : 아니요, **교대로 운전을 했기 때문에** 여행이 그렇게 피곤한 줄

몰랐어요.

No. Since we **took turns driving**, we did not find the trip too tiring.

029 교통 체증에 걸리다
be caught in the traffic

DIALOG

A : 왜 그렇게 늦었어요?

What took you so long?

B : **교통 체증에 걸렸어요.**

I was caught in the traffic.

030 교환하다
replace, exchange

DIALOG

A : 이 고장난 라디오를 **교환해** 주셨으면 해요.

I'd like you to **replace** this defective radio.

B : 보증 기간이 지나서 어쩔 수가 없네요.

The warranty has expired and there's nothing I can do about that.

[Note] defective 결점(결함)이 있는, 불비한/warranty (상품 품질 따위의) 담보 계약/expire 숨을 거두다, 죽다, (기간이) 만기가 되다, (권리 따위가) 소멸되다.

031 (상점에서) 구경만 하다
look around, browse

DIALOG

A : 무엇을 찾으시는지 도와드릴까요, 선생님?

Can I help you find something, sir?

B : 그냥 **구경만 하고** 있는 겁니다. 특별히 생각하고 있는 건 없어요.

I'm just **looking around**–nothing particular in mind.

[Note] looking around 대신에 browsing을 많이 사용한다.

032 구두쇠

cheapskate, penny pincher

DIALOG

A : 제가 **구두쇠**란 말씀인가요?

Are you saying that I'm a **cheapskate**?

B : 제 말 오해하지 마세요. 매우 검소하다는 뜻이에요.

Don't get me wrong. I just meant to say that you are very thrifty.

[Note] 구두쇠 a miser, a stingy person, a penny pincher

033 구조 변경을 하다

remodel

DIALOG

A : 이 집은 아주 구식이군요.

This house is very old fashioned.

B : 알아요. 내년에 **구조 변경을 하려고** 해요.

I know. We're going to **remodel** it next year.

034 구하다

get hold of, available

DIALOG

A : 그 책을 어디서 **구할 수 있나요**?

Where can I **get hold of** the book?

B : 시내 대부분의 상점에서 구할 수 있어요.

It is available at most of the stores in town.

035 군침이 돈다

My mouth waters.

DIALOG

A : 당신이 김치를 좋아하는 줄 알고 김치를 준비했어요.

We prepared kimchi for you. We know you like it.

B : 감사해요. 김치를 보니 **군침이 도는군요.**

Thank you. **My mouth waters** at the sight of kimchi.

[Note] at the sight of ~을 보니(보았을 때)/김치 생각을 하니 입에 군침이 도는군요. Thinking about kimchi makes my mouth water.

036 귀걸이

pierced, clip-on earring

DIALOG

A : 이 목걸이와 잘 어울리는 **귀걸이**를 좀 사고 싶어요.

I'd like some **earrings** to match this necklace.

B : **피어스트로** 할까요, **클립식으로** 할까요?

Do you want **pierced** or **clip-on earrings**?

037 귀띔해 주다

tip off

DIALOG

A : 그런 짓을 다시 하면 해고될 거예요.

You'll be fired if you do such a thing again.

B : **귀띔해 주셔서** 고마워요.

Thanks for **tipping** me **off**.

[Note] tip off 미리 정보를 알려 주다

038 그냥 넘어가다(처벌이나 징계받지 않고)

get away with it

DIALOG

A : 존은 제 시간에 사무실에 오는 법이 없어요. **그냥 두어서는 안 돼요.**

John never arrives at the office on time. **You shouldn't let her get away with it!**

B : 그렇지만 그의 마음을 상하게 하고 싶지는 않아요.

But I don't want to hurt her feelings.

039 그렇게만 하면 된다

That's all there is to it.

DIALOG

A : 제가 어떻게 하면 될까요?

What do you want me to do?

B : 침대에 누워 편안히 계세요. **그렇게만 하면 돼요.**

Just lay on the bed and relax. **That's all there's to it.**

040 그렇게 해 보다

Be my guest.

DIALOG

A : 아빠, 새 차 한 대 살까 해요.

I'm going to buy a new car, Dad.

B : 돈만 낼 수 있다면 **그렇게 하려무나.**

Be my guest if you think you can afford the payments.

041 긁어 부스럼 내다

open up a can of worms

DIALOG

A : 만일 그녀가 나를 계속 중상모략한다면, 언젠가는 따끔하게 한마디 해 줄 거야.

If she continues to slander me, some day I'm going to give her a piece of my mind.

B : **긁어 부스럼 내지 마세요.** 그냥 내버려 둬요.

Please **don't open up a can of worms.** Just let it go.

042 금상첨화

frosting (icing) on the cake

DIALOG

A : 직장은 어때요?

How do you like your job?

B : 월급도 많고 여름마다 유럽으로 무료 여행을 보내 주고 있어요.

Besides a high salary there is a free trip to Europe every summer.

A : **금상첨화군요.**

That's the **frosting on the cake.**

043 기고만장하다

go to one's head

DIALOG

A : **이 말 들었다고 기고만장하지 마세요.** 하지만 영어는 매우 훌륭해요.

Don't let this go to your head, but your English is very good.

B : 어쨌든 칭찬해 주셔서 감사합니다.

Anyway thank you for your compliment.

044 손님을 기다리다

expect company

DIALOG

A : **손님을 기다리고 있으니** 누군가 김 교수를 찾으면 나에게 안내해 주세요.

I'm expecting company. If someone asks for Professor Kim, please direct him to me.

B : 네, 선생님

Yes, sir.

045 기다리다 지치다

cool one's heels waiting for~

DIALOG

A : 두 시간 동안이나 **기다리느라 지쳤어요.**

I was **cooling my heels waiting for** you for two hours.

B : 오래 기다리게 해서 정말 미안해요.

I'm very sorry to have kept you waiting so long.

046 기록해 두다

keep track of~

DIALOG

A : 우리가 쓰는 돈을 다 **기록해 두어야 해요.**

We **should keep track of** every cent we spend.

B : 참 좋은 생각이에요.

That's a good idea.

047 기분을 상하게 하다

offend, hurt one's feelings

DIALOG

A : 당신 말씀이 마음에 들지 않아요.

I don't think I like your remarks.

B : 기분을 **상하게 해 드렸다면** 죄송합니다.

I'm sorry if I **offended** you.

[Note] 기분 나빠하지 마세요, 속옷이 보입니다.

Don't be offended, but your slip is showing.

048 기분좋게 해 주다

You've made my day.

DIALOG 1

A : 테니스 치러 가는 것이 어때요?

What about going to play tennis?

B : 당신 덕분에 아주 **기분이 좋습니다.** 이렇게 좋은 날씨에 집에 있는 것은 정말 싫어요.

You've made my day. I really hate being at home in this kind of nice weather.

DIALOG 2

A : 그 드레스 굉장히 아름답군요.

That's a very beautiful dress.

B : 감사합니다. **덕분에 기분이 아주 좋은데요.**

Thanks. **You've made my day.**

049 기운을 내다

cheer up

DIALOG 1

A : 오늘 기분이 우울해.

I'm in a blue mood.

B : **기운을 내.** 다 좋아질 거야

Cheer up. Things will get better.

DIALOG 2

A : 그녀는 남자 친구가 미국으로 떠난 후 줄곧 우울한 상태야.

She's been blue ever since her boy friend left for the United States.

B : 그녀는 너무 저기압이어서 우리가 하는 말이 **기운내게** 하는 데 도움이 안 될 것 같아.

She's so depressed that nothing we say seems to **cheer her up.**

[Note] blue 우울한(depressed, melancholy)

050 기일이 촉박하다

short notice

DIALOG

A : 우리가 주문한 거 늦어도 2주 안에 배달해 주세요.

You must deliver our order within two weeks at the latest.

B : **기일이 좀 촉박해요.** 빨라야 3주 안에 배달할 수 있어요.

That's a little **short notice**. We'll be able to deliver in three weeks at the earliest.

[Note] short notice 여유를 주지 않고 기일(시일)이 너무 촉박함.

051 기절하다(의식을 잃다)

pass out

DIALOG

A : 그는 **기절을 했어요.**

He **passed out.(He is unconscious.)**

B : 찬물을 좀 부어요. 그러면 의식이 돌아올 거예요.

Pour some cold water on him, and he'll come to.

052 기한이 넘었다

That's long overdue.

DIALOG

A : 나는 결국 자네가 추천한 그 대학에 응시하기로 결심했어.

I finally decided to apply for the college you recommended.

B : 벌써 했어야 했는데, **기한이 넘었네.**

It's about time you did that. **That's long overdue.**

053 기회를 놓치다

miss the boat

DIALOG

A : 그 회사의 제의를 거절했다는 거니? 단지 하나의 **기회를 놓친 것**

이 아니고 **일생에 한 번밖에 없는 좋은 기회를 놓친 거야.**

You mean you turned down the job offer from the company? You didn't just **miss the boat** : you **lost a once-in-a-lifetime chance.**

B : 알고 있어. 하지만 엎질러진 물을 한탄해 봤자 무슨 소용이 있겠어.

I know, but there's no use crying over spilled milk.

[Note] miss the boat 기회를 놓치다(lose an opportunity), (돌이킬 수 없는) 실패를 하다/turn down 거절하다(reject) : Henry tried to join the army but was turned down because of a weak heart. 헨리는 군에 입대하려고 했으나 심장이 약하다는 이유로 거절당했다.

054 (다음) 기회로 미루다

give you a rain check

DIALOG

A : 오늘 댁의 저녁 식사에 갈 수가 없습니다.

I can't come to your house for dinner.

B : 괜찮아요. **다음 기회로 미루지요.**

That's OK. I'll **give you a rain check.**

055 길이 엇갈리다

cross paths

DIALOG

A : 톰 봤니? 너 만나러 2층에 갔는데.

Did you see Tom? He went upstairs to see you.

B : 아니, **길이 엇갈린 모양이군.**

No, we must have **crossed paths.**

056 길들이다(길들다)
become (get) housebroken

DIALOG

A : 저 어린 망아지들은 훌륭한 말이 될 거예요.
Those young colts make wonderful horses.

B : 하지만 **길을 들여야 해요.**
But they **have to be housebroken.**

057 (맥주가) 김이 빠졌다
flat

DIALOG

A : 목이 마른데, 마실 것 좀 있나요?
I'm thirsty. Do you have something to drink?

B : 네, 먹다 남은 맥주가 냉장고에 있어요. 하지만 **김이 빠졌을지** 몰라요.
Yes, I have some leftover beer in the refrigerator, but I'm afraid it is **flat.**

[Note] 음료수가 김이 빠졌을 때는 flat을 쓰고 빵이 오래된 것이면 stale을 씀.

058 (~하는) 김에
while you're at it

DIALOG 1

A : 편지를 부치는 **김에** 내 편지도 좀 부쳐 줘요.
Please mail my letter too **while you are at it.**

B : 네, 부쳐 주고 말고요.
Sure.

DIALOG 2

A : 빌려 주는 **김에** 50달러 더 빌려 줄 수 있니?

Could you lend me 50 dollars more **while you are at it**?

B : 그런 식으로 내 우정을 이용하지 말게.

Don't take advantage of my friendship that way.

[Note] 같은 동작을 "~하는 김에" 할 때는 while you're at it란 표현을 씀.

059 까다롭다

1. 이것저것 너무 가리다

be choosy, be fussy

DIALOG

A : 아버지는 어머니가 만든 음식이 아니면 잡수시지 않는다.

My father refuses to eat any food not made by my mother.

B : 매우 **까다로우시군요.**

He's very **fussy(choosy)**.

2. 잔일에 너무 꼼꼼한

meticulous

DIALOG

A : 보고서를 제출하기 전에 중요한 숫자는 다시 확인해 보세요.

You'd better double-check the important figures before you hand in the report.

B : 네, 사장님이 숫자에 굉장히 **까다로우세요.**

Yes. The boss is very **meticulous** about figures.

3. 요구 사항이 많은
demanding

DIALOG

A : 집주인은 어때요?
What is the landlord like?

B : 꽤 **까다로운** 사람이에요.
He's really **demanding.**

4. 음식을 이것저것 가리는
finicky about food

DIALOG

A : 나의 형은 야채만 먹어요.
My brother eats only vegetables.

B : **음식에 까다로운** 모양이군요.
He seems to be very **finicky about food.**

A : 네, **까다로운 식성**을 가진 사람이지요.
Yes, he's a **picky eater.**

060 까마귀 나는 거리로(최단거리로)
as the crow flies

DIALOG

A : 그들 집과 당신 집과의 거리는 얼마나 되나요?
How far is their house from yours?

B : **최단거리로** 직접 가면 약 10마일입니다만, 물론 도로는 산들을 돌아야 하니 훨씬 더 멀지요.
Their house is about ten miles from ours, **as the crow flies** ; but of course the road is much longer since it winds around

the mountains.

061 깜빡 잊었다
slip one's mind

DIALOG

A : 그의 전화번호 좀 가르쳐 주세요.

Please give me his telephone number.

B : 알고 있는데 **깜빡 잊었어요.** 잠깐만요. 생각이 떠오를 거예요.

I know it, but it **slipped my mind**. Just a minute. It'll come to me.

062 (결국 ~로) 끝나다
end up

DIALOG

A : 좀 더 속력을 내세요.

Let's speed it up a little.

B : 안돼요. **딱지를 떼고 싶지 않아요.**

No. **I don't want to end up getting a ticket.**

063 (오늘은 이만) 끝냅시다
Let's call it a day.

DIALOG

A : 오늘은 많은 일을 했어요.

We have accomplished a great deal.

B : 저도 그렇게 생각해요. 오늘은 이만 **끝냅시다.**

I think so. **Let's call it** a day.

064 끝장나다(끝나다)

be through(with)~

DIALOG

A : 자네 미쳤나? 자네가 내게 이렇게 할 수는 없어.

Are you crazy? You can't do this to me.

B : 진정해, 친구. 어떻게 된 건지 설명할게.

Calm down, buddy. Let me explain **what really happened**.

A : 듣고 싶지 않아. **자네와 나는 끝났어!**

I don't want to hear it. **I'm through with you!**

065 끼어들지 마시오

You stay out of it.

DIALOG

A : 이것 봐. 그만들 싸워.

Come on. Stop fighting.

B : 넌 이 문제에 **끼어들지 마.**

You stay out of it.

나

066 나타나다(잃어버렸다고 생각한 물건이)
materialize

DIALOG

A : 어디서 그 펜을 찾았어요?
Where did you get the pen?

B : 잃어버렸다고 생각했는데 어느 날 책상 위에 **나타났어요.**
I thought I'd lost it, but it **materialized** on my desk one day.

067 날씬해지다
slim dowrn

DIALOG

A : 왜 식이요법을 하나요?
Why are you on a diet?

B : **날씬해지고 싶어서요.**
I want to slim down.

068 (~가 끝나고 ~가) 남다
to go

DIALOG 1

A : 몇 과를 마쳤니?
How many lessons did you finish?

B : 8과가 끝나고 3과가 **남았다.**
Eight down and three **to go**.

DIALOG 2

A : 얼마를 더 가야 하나요?

How much farther is it?

B : 글쎄요, 8마일 왔으니 2마일 더 **가야 해요.**

Well, eight down and two **to go**.

[Note] down 끝난(finished, done)

069 낯이 익다
look familiar

DIALOG 1

A : 실례합니다. **낯이 익은데,** 전에 어디선가 뵌 적이 없나요?

Excuse me. You **look familiar**. Haven't we met somewhere before?

B : 브리안의 생일 파티에서 뵌 듯하네요.

I think we met at Brian's birthday party.

A : 맞아요. 기억력이 좋군요.

That's right. You have a very good memory.

DIALOG 2

A : **낯이 익어 보이는군요.** 어디서 뵈었지요?

You look familiar. Where have I seen you?

B : 모르겠는데요.

Beats me.

[Note] Beats me 모르다(I don't know), 금시초문이다

070 냉대하다(쌀쌀한 태도를 보이다)
give (turn, show) a cold shoulder

DIALOG

A : 기분 나빠 보이는데, 무슨 일 있니?

You look down. Anything wrong?

B : 나는 정말 그 여자를 좋아하는데, 그 여자는 **나를 냉대해.**

I really like her, but she's **giving me the cold shoulder.**

071 냄새가 지독하다

give bad breath, have bad breath

DIALOG

A : 너 껌 씹고 있구나.

You are chewing gum now.

B : 그래. 입을 개운하게 해 줄 무엇이 필요해. 양파 수프 **냄새가 지독해.**

Yes. I need something to freshen my mouth. Onion soup **gives me bad breath.**

[Note] 입에서 악취가 나. You have bad breath./파슬리를 먹으면 입냄새가 없어진다. Parsley takes away bad breath./그녀 입에서 담배 냄새가 난다. Her breath smells of cigarette smoke.

072 넌더리나다(질렸다)

be fed up with~, be sick and tired of~

DIALOG

A : 그와 사이가 어때요?

How are you getting along with him?

B : 그의 게으름과 부주의에 **넌더리나요.**

I'm fed up with his laziness and carelessness.

[Note] be fed up with~ 넌더리나다, 싫증나다/I'm fed up with my wife. She nags too much about my drinking. 마누라에 넌더리가 나요. 술 마신다고 어떻게나 잔소리가 심하던지. (주) be fed up with~ 대신 be sick and tired of~를 사용해도 된다.

073 노발대발하다
hit the ceiling, blow one's top(lid)

DIALOG 1
A : 어제 저녁 무슨 일이 있었니?
Did anything happen to you last night?
B : 어제 저녁 내가 늦었어, 그랬더니 아버지께서 **노발대발하셨어.**
Last night I was late, and my father **hit the ceiling.**

DIALOG 2
A : 이것 큰일났는걸, 형의 차를 박살내 놓았으니.
Boy, I'm in trouble. I totaled my brother's car.
B : 알기만 하면 **노발대발할 거야.**
If he knew, he'd **blow his top.**

074 노예처럼 부려먹는 사람
a slave driver

DIALOG
A : 새로 온 사장 어때요?
How do you like your new boss?
B : 부하들을 **노예처럼 부려먹는 사람이에요.**
He is a **slave driver.**

075 노총각으로 지내다
play the field

DIALOG

A : 언제 결혼할 예정이에요?

When are you going to marry?

B : 아직 정착할 준비가 안 돼 여러 **여성과 데이트나 하고 지낼까 해요.**

I'm not ready to settle down yet, and I'd like to **play the field**.

[Note] play the field는 여러 여성과 데이트는 하면서 한 여자와 결혼하여 정착하지 않는 것을 말한다. (date many different girls and do not settle down with one person)

076 놀라게 하다

scare, shake up

DIALOG 1

A : 그가 어쨌기에 그러니?

What's wrong with him?

B : 그 바보 같은 사람이 어제 저녁 나를 굉장히 **놀라게 했어요.**

The stupid man nearly **frightened (scared)** me to death.

DIALOG 2

A : 어제 어머니께서 차 사고를 당하셨어요.

My mother was in a car accident yesterday.

B : 오, 저런! 괜찮으시니?

Oh, that's terrible. Is she OK?

A : 다치시지는 않았는데, **굉장히 놀라셨어요.**

She wasn't hurt, but she **was badly shaken up**.

[Note] be frightened (scared) to death "놀라 죽다"에서 "굉장히 놀라다"/shake up (신경을) 건드리다, 오싹하게 하다, 충격을 주다/She was shaken up by the bad news. 그 좋지 않은 소식에 충격을 받았다.

077 놀리다(농담하다)
pull one's leg, put one on, kid

DIALOG 1

A : 그의 부인이 세 쌍둥이를 낳았어요.
His wife had triplets!

B : **놀리려고** 그러는 거지요.
You must **be pulling my leg.** (You must be **kidding.**)

A : 아니요, 정말입니다.
No. I'm serious.

DIALOG 2

A : 저는 아이가 15명이에요.
I have fifteen children.

B : 날 **놀리시는군요.**
You're **putting me on.**

[Note] kidding의 발음은 '키링'으로 들리게 한다.

078 누워서 떡먹기
It's a piece of cake, It's a cinch(snap).

DIALOG

A : 도대체 젓가락 사용하는 법을 어떻게 배웠어요?
How in the world did you learn to use chopsticks?

B : **누워서 떡먹기처럼 쉬워요.**
It's a piece of cake.

079 눈이 위(胃)보다 크다
Your eyes are bigger than your stomach.

DIALOG

A : 다 먹을 수가 없어요.

I can't eat all of the food.

B : 당신 **눈이** 당신 배보다 더 크군요.

Your **eyes** are bigger than your stomach.

[Note] Your eyes are bigger than your stomach은 매우 재미 있는 표현이다. 뷔페 같은 데서 잔뜩 가지고 왔다가 다 처리하지 못하고 음식을 많이 남길 때 사용할 수 있는 표현이다.

080 눈에 잘 띄는 건물

landmark, most prominent building

DIALOG

A : 사무실 건물을 어떻게 찾을 수 있을까요?

How can I find your office building?

B : 근처에 강남구청이 있어요. **눈에 잘 띄는 건물이에요.**

There's Kangnam District Office building near it. It's a **landmark**.

081 눈에 눈곱이 끼다

matter in the corner of your eyes

DIALOG

A : 내 얼굴을 왜 쳐다보는 거야?

Why are you staring at my face?

B : **눈에 눈곱이 꼈네요.** 닦으세요.

You have matter in the corner of your eyes. Wipe your eyes.

082 눈물이 나다

My eyes are watering

DIALOG

A : 눈이 왜 그래요?

What's wrong with your eyes?

B : 바람이 심하게 불어 **눈물이 나네요.**

The wind is blowing so bad that **my eyes are watering.**

083 눈 뜨자마자

first thing in the morning

DIALOG

A : 제임스는 줄담배를 피웁니다. 하루 평균 두 갑을 피우지요.

James is a real chain-smoker. He smokes two packs a day on the average.

B : 알아요. 그는 아침에 **눈 뜨자마자** 담배를 피우고 밤에도 마지막으로 담배를 피우고 잠자리에 들지요.

I know. He smokes **the first thing** in the morning and the last thing at night.

[Note] on the average 평균적으로, 대략

다

084 다녀오다(잠깐)

be gone, take a short trip to~

DIALOG

A : 시카고에 잠깐 다녀올까 해요.

I'm going to take a short trip to Chicago.

B : 언제 떠나시나요?

When are you leaving?

085 심하게 다루지 않다

go easy

DIALOG

A : 그 코치 사람이 어때요?

How is the coach?

B : 그는 참 좋은 사람이야. 팀이 졌지만 심하게 다루지 않았어.

He's a very nice person. His team lost but he **went easy** on them.

[Note] go easy 편안(태평)하게 해나가다, (상대방에게) 부담감을 갖지 않게 하다/I'll go easy on you. Let's play a game. 천천히 할 테니 한 게임 합시다.

086 다행이다

It's a good thing. Good for you!

DIALOG 1

A : 이 드레스 정말 비싸군요.

This dress is really expensive.

B : 제가 여웃돈을 가져와서 정말 **다행이군요.**

It's a good thing I brought some extra money.

DIALOG 2

A : 그것이 바로 제가 좋아하는 종류예요.

That's just the kind I like.

B : 다행이군요!

Good for you!

087 단것을 좋아하다

have a sweet tooth

DIALOG

A : 제인은 사탕을 좋아하나요?

Does Jane like candy?

B : 네, 그녀는 **단것을 좋아해서** 사탕을 거절하는 법이 없어요.

Yes, she **has such a sweet tooth** that she never refuses candy.

088 단골 손님

regular customer

DIALOG

A : 이거 수선하는 데 얼마나 들까요?

How much would it cost me to fix it?

B : **단골 손님**이니 돈을 안 받겠어요.

Since you are a **regular customer**, there will be no charge on it.

089 (바지) 단추가 열려 있군요

Your fly is open.

DIALOG

A : 기분 나쁘게 생각지 마세요. 바지 **단추가** 열려 있어요.

Don't get offended. Your **fly** is open.

B : 감사합니다.

Thank you.

[Note] "바지 단추가 열려 있군요"를 한영사전에는 "Your fly button is open."이라고 되어 있는데 button을 사용하지 말 것. 그리고 "Your stable door is open."도 사용하지 않는다.

090 달걀을 어떻게 해 드릴까요?

How would you like your eggs?

DIALOG

A : **달걀을 어떻게 해 드릴까요**? 우리는 poached, scrambled, over easy(hard), sunny side up 그리고 hard boiled와 soft boiled가 있습니다.

How would you like your eggs? We have poached, scrambled, over easy, sunny side up, hard boiled and soft boiled.

B : Over easy로 해 주세요.

Over easy, please.

[Note] "달걀 한 판"은 one gross of eggs

한 판을 다 사면 싸게 해 드려요. If you buy one gross, I'll give you a discount.

091 달팽이 걸음을 하다

move at a snail's pace

DIALOG

A : 눈 때문에 길이 미끄러울 거예요.

The snow will make the roads slippery.

B : 그러면 차들이 **달팽이 걸음을 하게 되겠군요.**

Then the traffic will **move at a snail's pace.**

092 (꼭) 닮았다

as alike as two peas in a pod

DIALOG 1

A : 외모나 태도에 있어서 두 형제는 **꼭 닮았어요.**

In both appearance and manner, the two brothers are **as alike as two peas in a pod.**

B : 그러면 누가 누군지 잘 모르겠군요.

Then it must be very hard to tell one from the other.

[Note] "꼭 닮았다"는 identical을 사용할 수도 있다.

DIALOG 2

A : 그는 쌍둥이 형이 있어요.

He has a twin brother.

B : 그래요? 그들은 꼭 닮았나요?

Really? Are they **identical**?

093 당황하다

panic, embarrass

DIALOG 1

A : **당황하지 마세요.** 침착하세요.

Just don't panic. Calm down.

B : 그들이 당신을 데리러 2~3분 후에 올 겁니다.

They will pick you up in a few minutes.

DIALOG 2

A : 꼬마가 설교 도중에 울기 시작했어요.

My kid started to cry in the middle of preach.

B : 얼마나 **당황하셨겠어요!** 그래 어떻게 하셨어요?

How embarrassing! So what did you do?

[Note] panic은 '공포에 질리다, 겁을 집어먹다'이고, embarrass는 '난처하게 하다, 쩔쩔매게 하다'의 뜻이니 사용되는 경우가 다름에 주의할 것. How embarrassing!은 아이의 울음이 얼마나 당신을 당황하게 만들었겠느냐의 뜻이다.

094 대소변을 가리다

be housebroken

DIALOG 1

A : 귀여운 개를 갖고 있군요. 암컷이에요, 수컷이에요?

You've got a cute dog there. Is that a he or a she?

B : 암컷이에요.

It's a she.

DIALOG 2

A : 대소변을 가리겠죠?

She **is housebroken**, isn't she?

B : 아직도 잘 못 가려요. 훈련 중이에요.

Not quite yet. I'm still training her.

095 따끔하게 혼내 주다

give someone a piece of one's mind

DIALOG

A : 그것에 대해 그에게 **따끔하게 한마디해야겠다.**

I'm going to **give him a piece of my mind** about that.

B : 소란스럽게 하지 마세요. 그냥 내버려 두시지요.

Don't make a scene. Why don't you let it go?

[**Note**] make a scene 야단법석을 떨다, 소란을 피우다.

096 따지다

give someone a piece of one's mind

DIALOG

A : 나는 이 형편없는 기숙사 식사에 신물이 나요. 이제 더이상 참을 수가 없어요.

I'm sick and tired of this lousy dorm food. Enough is enough.

B : 지배인에게 좀 **따지시지요.**

Why don't you **give** the manager **a piece of your mind**?

097 딸려오다

come with~

DIALOG

A : 그거 얼마에 샀어요?

How much was it?

B : 산 것이 아니고 컴퓨터 살 때 **딸려온** 거예요.

I didn't pay for it. It **came with** the computer.

098 더위를 쫓다(잊다)

beat the heat

DIALOG

A : 더위를 어떻게 참습니까?

How can you stand the heat?

B : 에어컨으로 **더위를 쫓고 있어요.** 시원하고 상쾌하게 해 주거든요.

We **beat the heat** with the air-conditioner. It keeps us cool and refreshed.

099 (요리가) 덜 익은

undercooked

DIALOG

A : 이 고기는 왜 이렇게 질기지요?

Why is this meat so tough?

B : **덜 익었어요.** 좀 더 오래 요리했어야 했는데.

It's **undercooked.** It should have been cooked longer.

100 덤으로 주는 것

a free gift

DIALOG

A : 그거 얼마예요?

How much do you charge for it?

B : 아니요, **덤으로 주는** 거예요.

No, This is **a free gift.**

101 데우다

warm up

DIALOG 1

A : 언제 점심 드실 거예요?

When are we going to have lunch?

B : 이 국을 **데우는 대로** 간단히 합시다.

As soon as I **warm up** this soup, we will have a little lunch.

DIALOG 2

A : 시간이 많지 않아요.

We don't have much time.

B : 냉동식품 몇 가지를 **데우지요.**

Why don't we **warm up** a couple of frozen dinners?

102 도보 여행을 하다

take a walking tour of~

DIALOG

A : 시내를 **도보 여행하려고 하는데요.**

I want to **take a walking tour of** the city.

B : 좋은 생각이에요. 그런데 안내자를 고용해야 될 거예요. 제가 소개해 드릴까요?

Good idea. But you'll need a guide. Shall I make arrangements for you?

103 도착 예정이다

be due here

DIALOG

A : 비행기가 7시 **도착 예정인데** 벌써 7시 10분이에요. 이미 10분 연착이군요.

The plane **is due here** at seven, but it's already seven-ten.

It's already ten minutes overdue.

B : 하지만 염려 마세요. 곧 도착할 거예요. 10분 늦는 것은 정상이지요.

But don't worry. It'll be arriving any minute now.

Ten minutes'delay is normal.

104 돌아다니다
move around, be on the move

DIALOG

A : 그가 당신에게 전화하기를 원하세요?
Would you like him to call you back?

B : 아니요, 저는 지금 나와서 **돌아다니고 있어요.** 나중에 제가 다시 전화할게요.
No, **I'm moving around** right now, so I think I'll call back later.

105 동전을 던져 결정하다
flip a coin

DIALOG

A : 오늘 저녁에 뭘 할까요? 영화 보러 갈까요, 공부를 할까요?
What shall we do tonight–go to the movies or study?

B : **동전을 던져 결정합시다.** 앞쪽이 나오면 영화 보러 가고, 뒷면이 나오면 공부하기로.
Let's flip a coin. If it's heads, we go to the movies. If it's tails, we study.

[Note] flip the pages 책장을 넘기다/heads (보통 pl.) (두 사람이 있는) 화폐의 표면(opp. tails)/Heads or tails? 앞이냐 뒤냐? (돈을 던져 승부를 가릴 때 쓰는 말), As a joke we sometimes say. "Heads I win tails you lose!" "표면이 나오면 내가 이기고 뒷면이 나오면 자네가 지는 거야!"라고 종종 농담하기도 한다.

106 돼지우리 같군
It looks like a pig-pen.

DIALOG

A : 이 방은 더럽고 엉망이군.

This room is a mess!

B : 정말 그래요. **꼭 돼지우리 같아요.**

It sure is. **It looks like a pig-pen.**

107 가슴이 두근거리다(초조해하다)

I have butterflies in my stomach.

DIALOG

A : 그렇게 초조해하지 말아요. 잘 해낼 거예요.

Don't be so nervous. You'll do fine.

B : **가슴이 두근거려서 못 견디겠어요.**

I have butterflies in my stomach.

[Note] a social butterfly 사교로 분주한 사람/You are a social butterfly.

108 두통거리

a pain in the neck

DIALOG

A : 당신 부인과는 사이가 어때요?

How are you getting along with your wife?

B : 내 아내는 정말 **두통거리예요.** 항상 바가지를 긁어요.

My wife is **a pain in the neck.** She's always nagging at me.

[Note] nag 바가지 긁다/우리 교장은 정말 두통거리야. 나를 못살게 굴거든. My principal is a pain in the neck. He's always picking on me.

109 둘러보다

make a tour of~

DIALOG

A : 그분이 집을 한번 죽 **둘러보게** 해 드려.

Give him **the grand tour of** the house.

B : 꽤 큰 거실이 있군요.

It has a rather large living room.

110 뒤죽박죽이다

all mixed up

DIALOG

A : 왜 리포트를 제출하지 않나요?

Why don't you hand in the report?

B : 정리를 해야 해요. 페이지들이 **뒤죽박죽이거든요.**

I have to organize it. I got the pages **all mixed up.**

111 드레싱

dressing

DIALOG

A : 샐러드에 어떤 **드레싱을** 치시겠어요?

What kind of **dressing** would you like on your salad?

B : 어떤 종류가 있나요 ?

What kind do you have?

112 들르다

Let's come by.

DIALOG

A : 그녀는 매우 울적해하고 있어요. 좋아하는 언니가 세상을 떠났거든요.

She's very upset. Her favorite sister passed away yesterday.

B : 내일 **들러서** 위로해 줍시다.

Let's **come by** tomorrow to cheer her up.

[**Note**] pass away 세상을 떠나다(die)/cheer up 위로하다, 기운을 내다

113 마음대로 하세요(좋으실 대로 하세요)
Suit yourself.

DIALOG

A : 코트를 벗어도 될까요?
Do you mind if I take off my coat?

B : 네, **마음대로 하세요.**
No, I don't mind. **Suit yourself.**

114 마음에 걸리다
weigh on one's mind

DIALOG

A : 시험이 항상 **마음에 걸리네요.**
Examinations **weigh on my mind** all the time.

B : 마음을 느긋하게 가지세요
Please relax.

115 마음 졸이게 하다
keep one in suspense

DIALOG

A : **나를 마음 졸이게 하지 마세요.** 그 속에 무엇이 있나요?
Don't keep me in suspense. What's in it?

B : 당신을 놀라게 해 줄 것을 갖고 있지요.
I have a surprise for you.

116 막상막하
neck and neck(= close)

DIALOG 1

A : 테니스 시합은 비등했나요?

Was the tennis game close?

B : 그랬어요. 정말 **막상막하였어요.**

Sure was. It was **neck and neck.**

DIALOG 2

A : 누가 시장 선거에서 이겼어요?

Who won the mayoral race?

B : **당락을 판가름하기 어려울 정도로 백중세예요.**

It's still **too close to call.**(= It cannot be judged or predicted.)

117 말짱하다
be in great shape

DIALOG

A : 이 차값으로 얼마나 요구하는데요?

How much are you asking for this car?

B : 아시다시피 **그 차는 아주 멀쩡해요.**

You know, **it's in great shape.**

[Note] "말짱하다"는 경우에 따라서 complete, flawless, perfect, be free from damage 또는 be in perfect condition으로 사용할 수 있다. "정신이 말짱하다"는 have a clear mind, be sound in mind 또는 be sane을 사용한다.

118 (내) 맘을 어찌 그렇게 잘 알지요
You read my mind.

DIALOG

A : 커피 한잔 하실까요?

Would you care for a cup of coffee?

B : **어쩌면 내 마음을 그렇게 잘 알지요**?

You read my mind.

119 맛이 어때요?

What's it taste like?

DIALOG

A : 인삼차를 마셔 본 적 있나요?

Have you ever tried ginseng tea?

B : 아니요, **맛이 어때요**?

No, **what's it taste like**?

120 맛이 이상하다

It tastes funny, It doesn't taste right.

DIALOG

A : 햄버거가 좀 이상해요.

Something is wrong with the hamburg.

B : 네, **맛이 이상한데요.**

Yes, **it doesn't taste right.**

121 망쳐 버리다

ruin, mess up

DIALOG 1

A : 소문이 나면 일을 **망쳐 버릴지도** 몰라요.

Rumors may **ruin** the whole thing.

B : 나는 입이 가벼운 사람이 아니에요.

I'm not a blabber-mouth.

DIALOG 2

A : 집 페인트 칠은 어떻게 되어 가나요?

How is your house painting coming along?

B : **망쳐 버렸어요.** 종류를 잘못 사용해서요.

I messed it up. (혹은 I goofed it up.)

I used the wrong kind of paint.

[Note] goof up 큰 실수를 하다/I could have won, but I goofed up. 이길 수 있었는데 실수를 해 버렸어.

122 (물건을) 맡기다 (꼬리표를 받고)

check

DIALOG

A : 안으로 들어가기 전에 **코트를 맡깁시다.**

Why don't we **check our coats** before going inside?

B : 좋은 생각이에요. 보관소 여직원한테 표를 받으세요.

Good idea. Get the token from the cloak girl.

[Note] cloak room (호텔, 극장, 식당 따위의) 외투(휴대품) 보관소

123 (병)맥주와 (생)맥주

bottle beer and draft beer

DIALOG

A : 맥주를 마시는 게 어때요?

How does beer sound?

B : **(병)맥주와 (생)맥주**가 있어요.

We have **bottle beer and draft on tap.**

A : 전부 **(생)맥주**로 주세요.

We'll have a round of your **draft beer.**

[Note] draft beer 생맥주/on tap (통에) 따르는 꼭지가 달린.

124 머리 손질을 하다
have one's hair done

DIALOG

A : 와! 오늘 근사한데요.

Wow! You look great today!

B : 고마워요. 행사를 위해 **머리 손질을 하고** 새 드레스를 샀어요.

Thanks. **I had my hair done** and bought a new dress for the occasion.

[Note] hair-do 머리 모양

125 머리가 깨어질 듯 아프다
My head is killing me.
= I have a splitting headache.

DIALOG

A : 지겨운 날이군! **머리가 깨어질 듯 아프군요.**

What a day! **My head is killing me.**

B : 너무 열심히 일을 하고 있어요. 좀 쉬셔야겠어요.

You've been working too hard. You should relax a little.

126 먹다 남은 것
left-overs

DIALOG

A : 이 음식 이디서 났니?

Where did you get this food?

B : 지난 토요일 모임에서 **먹다 남은 거야.**

This is **leftovers** from the get-together last Saturday.

[Note] get-together 모임, 간담회/left over는 형용사로서 '먹다 남은'

127 (남의 재산을) 먹어치우다
eat a person out of house and home

DIALOG

A : 우리는 야생동물처럼 식성이 좋은 아들이 둘 있어요.

We have two young sons with appetite like wild animals.

B : 꼭 말처럼 많이 먹겠군요.

They must eat like a horse.

A : **그 애들은 우리 재산을 다 먹어 없애 버릴 거예요.**

They'll eat us out of house and home.

[Note] 당신은 냉장고에 있는 음식을 다 먹어치웠어. You emptied my refrigerator. = You ate me out of house and home.

128 멋있는
gorgeous, stunning, look like a million dollars!

DIALOG 1

A : 그 드레스 정말 **멋있어요. 아주 멋있는데요!**

That drcss is **gorgeous. You look like a million dollars!**

B : 칭찬해 주셔서 고마워요.

Thank you for your compliment.

DIALOG 2

A : 정말 멋있어요. 당장 보여 드리고 싶군요.

It's a real beauty. I can't wait to show it to you.

B : 정말 **멋있는데요.** 비싸겠군요.

It's really **stunning.** It cost a fortune.

[Note] stunning 기절시키는, 깜짝 놀랄 만한, 어리둥절하게 만드는/cost a fortune 굉장히 비싸다.

129 메뉴가 굉장하군요

The menu is enormous.

DIALOG

A : 이곳 음식 정말 마음에 들 거예요.

You'll really like the food here.

B : **메뉴가 굉장하군요.**

The menu is enormous.

A : 네, 훌륭한 음식이 많이 있어요. 뭐든지 말씀만 하세요. 아마 다 있을 거예요.

Yes, they have an excellent selection. You name it and they probably have it.

130 모험을 하다

take a chance

DIALOG

A : 어느 대학에 입학 원서를 내려고 하니?

What universities are you going to apply to?

B : 서울대와 연세대에요.

Seoul and Yonsei, of course.

A : **큰 모험을 하고 있다**는 생각이 드는구나. 다소 경쟁이 낮은 대학을 정하는 것이 어때?

I'm afraid you're **taking a big chance.**

Why don't you settle for something less competitive instead of **taking a chance**?

[Note] settle for~ = ~로 만족하다(be content with~)/competitive 경쟁의, 경쟁으로 결정되는

131 목이 심하게 아프다

have a sore throat

DIALOG

A : 열이 있는 데다 **목이 심하게 아프고** 침을 삼킬 수가 없어요.

I've been running a fever and I **have a sore throat.**

It's so sore I can hardly swallow.

B : 처방을 해 드릴 테니 동네 약국에서 약을 지으세요.

I'll give you a prescription that you can have filled at your local drug store.

[Note] run a fever 열이 나다(run a temperature)/fill a prescription 처방대로 약을 짓다(prepare medicine according to a prescription)

132 목이 쉰

hoarse

DIALOG 1

A : 목이 아프세요?

Is your throat sore?

B : 아니요, 감기로 **목이 좀 쉬었어요.**

No, but I'm a little **hoarse** from a cold.

[Note] "목이 쉬다"는 have a hoarse throat나 have a frog in one's throat 또는 be hoarse라고도 한다.

DIALOG 2

A : 자네 **목이 쉰 것 같은데.**

You **sound** a little **hoarse.**

B : 감기가 든 것 같아요. 어제 비 오는데 밖에 있었거든요.

I'm coming down with a cold. I was out in the rain yesterday.

[Note] come down with~ (병 따위) ~의 기운이 들다

133 목적지에 거의 다 왔나요?

Are we almost there?

DIALOG

A : **거의 다 왔나요?**

Are we almost there?

B : 아니요, 하지만 절반은 더 왔어요.

No, but we're more than half way.

134 몸만 오세요

bring yourself

DIALOG

A : 뭘 좀 가지고 올게요. 저도 조금은 분담하고 싶어요.

Let me bring something. I'd like to chip in, too.

B : **그냥 몸만 오세요.** 제가 샌드위치와 그 외 필요한 것도 준비할게요.

Just bring yourself. I'll have sandwiches and whatever else we need.

[Note] chip in 공헌하다, 기부하다, 한몫들다(join in)/They all chipped in to buy it. 그들은 모두 그것을 사기 위하여 얼마씩 기부했다. Everyone in the office chipped in a dollar to buy Mary a wedding present. 사무실에 있는 사람들은 마리에게 결혼 선물을 사주는 데 모두 1달러씩 보탰다.

135 몸이 불편하다

feel under the weather

DIALOG

A : 미안하지만 약속을 지키지 못할 것 같아요.

Sorry, but I'm going to have to break our date.

B : 왜요, 무슨 일인데요?

Why, what's the matter?

A : **몸이 좀 불편해서요.**

I'm feeling under the weather.

136 몸살이 나다

I ache all over.

DIALOG

A : 어제 조깅을 시작했는데 **온몸이 쑤시고 아파요.**

I just started jogging yesterday and **I ache all over.**

B : 하지만 곧 사라질 거예요.

But it goes away soon.

137 못살게 하다

pick on a person, give a hard time

DIALOG

A : 나를 **못살게 하지 말고** 좀 내버려둬요.

Stop **picking on** me.

B : 너는 지저분한 사람이야. 너의 방은 돼지우리야.

You're a messy person. Your room is a pig pen.

[Note] "나를 못살게 하지 말아요"할 때 "Would you get off my back?"이라고도 한다.

138 몽땅 다(모두, 전부)

the works

DIALOG 1

A : 핫도그를 어떻게 해 드릴까요?

How do you like your hot dog?

B : 있는 것 **모두 주세요.**

I want everything on it, **the works.**

DIALOG 2

A : 20불에 무엇을 해 주나요?

What do you do for $20?

B : 오일 교환, 그리스, 오일필터 교환 등 **몽땅 해** 드려요.

An oil change, grease job, new filter, **the works.**

139 무(無)에서 다시 시작하다

start from scratch

DIALOG

A : 그 폭풍이 우리 집을 완전히 파괴해 버렸어.
우리는 집을 다시 짓고 **무에서 시작해야 해.**
That tornado destroyed our house completely.
We have to **start from scratch** rebuilding our house.

B : 참 안됐군요. **무에서 시작한다**는 것이 쉽지 않은 일인데.
That's too bad. It's not easy to **start from scratch.**

[Note] tornado 미국에서 4~6월 사이에 미시시피 강 유역 지방에서 발생하는 맹렬한 폭풍.

140 무료

no charge, on the house

DIALOG 1

A : 시험해 보는 것은 **무료예요.**
There's **no charge for** a trial.

B : 얼마 동안 그 기계를 시험해 볼 수 있나요?
How long can I keep the machine on trial?

DIALOG 2

A : 이 술은 **무료로** 드리는 거예요.
This drink is **on the house.**

B : 감사합니다.
Thank you.

A : 천만에요.
You're welcome.

[Note] on the house 공짜로, 사업주 지불로(free to the customer)

141 무료 편승하다
hitchhike

DIALOG

A : 기름이 다 떨어졌어요.
We're out of gas.

B : **무료 편승해야겠어요.**
We have to **hitchhike.**

[Note] hitchhike 지나가는 자동차를 가끔 얻어타며 도보 여행하다, 자동차 편승 여행

142 무사하다(처벌받지 않고)
get away with it

DIALOG

A : 그는 좋은 순경이었어. 딱지를 떼지 않았어.
He was a nice cop. He didn't give me a ticket.

B : 자네가 **무사할 수 있었던** 건 운이 좋기 때문이야.
You were just lucky to **get away with it.**

143 무승부로 끝나다
It was a draw(tie). (It ended in a draw.)

DIALOG

A : 레슬링 시합은 어떻게 되었나요?
How did the wrestling match turn out?

B : **무승부로 끝났어요.**
It was a draw. (It ended in a draw.)

[Note] 무승부 tie, draw.

144 문이 잠겨 들어가지 못하다
be locked out of~, lock oneself out of~

DIALOG

A : 왜 밖에 계세요?

Why do you stay out?

B : **문이 잠겨 들어가지 못하고 있어요.**

I accidentally **locked myself out of the house.**

[Note] 열쇠를 안에 두고 문을 잠갔을 때 be locked out of~ 혹은 locked oneself out of~라 한다. I locked myself out of the car. 차 안에 열쇠를 두고 잠가 버려 들어가지 못하고 있어.

145 문제가 생기다
be in trouble

DIALOG

A : **큰 문제가 생겼어.** 차 안에 열쇠를 두고 문을 잠가 버렸어.

We're in big trouble. We locked ourselves out of the car.

B : 걱정 마세요. 안전을 위하여 여분 열쇠를 가지고 다니니까요.

Don't worry, I carry an extra key just to be on the safe side.

146 (손에서) 미끄러지다
slip out of one's hand

DIALOG

A : 네가 그 문을 고의로 쾅 닫았니?

Did you slam that door on purpose?

B : 아니요. 손에서 **미끄러졌어요.**

No. It **slipped** out of my hand.

147 미소를 띠다
wear a smile

DIALOG

A : 나는 저 친구의 거만한 **미소가** 싫어요.

I don't like that arrogant **smile he's wearing.**

B : 나는 저 친구의 **콧수염이** 싫어요.

I don't like the **mustache he's wearing.**

[Note] wear의 사용에 유의할 것. (수염을) 기르고 있다, (미소를) 띠고 있다, (향수를) 바르고 있다. What's that perfume you're wearing? 네가 바른 향수는 어떤 거야?

148 미정이다
It's up in the air.

DIALOG

A : 곧 미국에 갈 거라고 하던데 사실이에요?

Is it true that you're going to the States soon?

B : 글쎄요, **아직 미정이에요.**

Well, **it's still up in the air.**

[Note] up in the air 미정이다(undecided)/Our plans for a vacation are still up in the air. 방학 계획은 아직 미정이다.

149 미치게 하다
drive someone crazy

DIALOG 1

A : 저 애들 꽤 시끄러워요.

The children are very noisy.

B : 네, 정말 **시끄러워 미치겠어요.**

Yes, **they're driving me crazy!**

DIALOG 2

A : 당신 다이어트 하나요?

Are you on a diet?

B : 네, 이 다이어트 때문에 **미치겠어요.**

Yes, this diet is **driving me crazy.**

A : 그걸 끝까지 지키기만 하면 곧 날씬해질 거예요.

You'll be thin in no time if you stick to it.

[Note] be on a diet 다이어트하다/No pie for me, I'm on a diet. 저는 파이를 안 먹어요, 다이어트 중이에요/in no time 곧(soon)/stick to~ 끝까지 ~를 고수하다.

150 (~에) 미쳐 있다(몹시 좋아하다)

be crazy about

DIALOG

A : 그녀가 그를 빤히 쳐다보고 있는 것 좀 보세요.

Look at how she's staring at him.

B : **그에게 미쳐 있는** 게 확실해요.

It's pretty obvious **she's crazy about him,** isn't it?

151 믿긴 어렵겠지만

Believe it or not

DIALOG

A : 저 까다로운 노인을 어떻게 참으세요?

How can you stand that cranky old man?

B : **믿긴 어렵겠지만** 그분이 저의 최고 고객 중 한 분이에요.

Believe it or not, he's one of my best customers.

152 그대로 믿다(속다)

take in

DIALOG 1

A : 왜 그를 믿었어요?

Why did you believe him?

B : 그의 상냥한 예의와 세련된 대화 태도 때문에 **그냥 믿었지요.**

We **were** all **taken in** by his smooth manner and polished way of talking.

DIALOG 2

A : 왜 그 형편없는 영화를 보러 갔어요?

Why did you go to that terrible movie?

B : 광고를 **그대로 믿었지요.**

I **was taken in** by the advertisement.

153 말을 믿다

take one's word

DIALOG

A : 어떤 부작용도 없으리라는 것을 보장해 드리죠.

I guarantee you won't have any side effects.

B : 그것에 대해 저는 아무것도 모르니 선생님 **말씀만 믿겠어요.**

I'll have to **take your word** for it since I don't know anything about it.

154 밀려 있다(일, 집세 등)

be behind in

DIALOG 1

A : **일이 하도 밀려 있어** 처리하려면 며칠은 걸릴 거야.

I'm so behind in my work, it'll take several days to catch up.

B : 도와드릴 수 있을 거예요.

Maybe I can help you.

DIALOG 2

A : 톰이 집세를 못 내고 **밀려 있다는데.**

I hear Tom **is behind in** his rent.

B : 그거 정말 안됐군요.

That's a shame.

[Note] "참 안됐다"를 "That's too bad."라고 하면 너무 정중한(겸손한) 표현이다. "That's a shame."을 흔히 사용한다.

바

155 바람을 맞히다

stand someone up

DIALOG

A : 자네 여자 친구가 왜 그렇게 화를 내지?

Why is your girl friend so mad at you?

B : 어제 저녁에 **바람을 맞힌 데다가** 다른 여자와 데이트하는 것을 들켰거든.

I **stood her up** last night and she caught me dating another girl.

A : 그래? 그건 너무 지나쳤다고 생각지 않니?

Oh, yeah? Don't you think that's going too far?

[Note] be mad at + 사람 (~에게) 화내다/go too far 너무 지나치다

156 바람부는 대로 하겠다

play it by ear

DIALOG

A : 갈 곳을 결정했니?

Have you decided where you're going?

B : 거기에 도착하면 **바람부는 대로 할 거야.**

I'll play it by ear when I get there.

A : 즐거운 여행 되길 바래.

Well, I hope you have a good trip.

157 바람을 쏘이다(물건을)

air out

DIALOG

A : 이 담요 냄새가 지독한데 **바람을 쏘여야겠어요.**

This blanket smells terrible. We'd better **air** it **out**.

B : **바람을 쏘이는 것**보다 빨아야겠어요.

It needs washing instead of **airing**.

158 바빠서 꼼짝 못하다

be tied up, have one's hands full

DIALOG 1

A : 가서 뵈올 수 있을까요?

Can I come over and see you?

B : 7시까지는 **바빠서** 사무실에 **꼼짝 못하고 있어야** 해요.

I'll **be tied up** at the office until seven o'clock.

DIALOG 2

A : 바쁘신가요?

Are you busy?

B : 네, **바빠요.**

Yes, **my hands** are **full**.

159 박수를 보내다

give one a big hand

DIALOG

A : 그 공연은 선풍적이었어요.

The performance was sensational.

B : 그들에게 **박수를 보냅시다.**

Let's **give them a big hand.**

[Note] give one a (big) hand = applaud(enthusiastically and at length), 그녀가 노래를 불렀을 때 청중들은 그녀에게 박수를 보냈다. After she finished singing, the audience gave her a big hand./get a standing ovation(혹은 get an ovation) 기립 박수를 받다.

160 (돈을) 반환하다

refund

DIALOG

A : 이 스웨터를 돈으로 **반환해** 주실 수 있나요?

Can I **have a refund** on this sweater?

B : 안 됩니다. 그렇게 해 드릴 수 없어요.

No, I'm afraid we can't do that.

161 발목을 삐다

sprain one's ankle

DIALOG

A : 어떻게 된 일이에요?

What did you do to yourself?

B : 발목을 **삐었어요.**

I sprained my ankle.

162 발이 저리다

one's leg (foot) is asleep

DIALOG

A : 왜 발을 계속 움직이고 있어요?

Why do you keep moving your foot?

B : 발이 **저려서요.**

It's asleep.

163 밤샘을 하다

stay up all night

DIALOG

A : 파티 재미있었어요?

Did you have a good time at the party?

B : 네, 카드놀이하면서 **밤샘을 했어요.**

Yes. **We stayed up all night** playing cards.

164 밤이 이르다

The night is still young.

DIALOG

A : 좀 더 계시지요. **밤이 아직 이른데요.**

Why don't you stay awhile? **The night is still young.**

B : 아니요, 가봐야겠어요. 내일 아침 일찍 일어나야 해요.

No. I'd better be going. I have to get up early tomorrow morning.

165 밤참

a midnight snack

DIALOG

A : 저녁으로 뭘 드시겠어요?

What are you going to have for dinner?

B : 저녁은 거르고 **밤참으로** 밀크쉐이크를 하나 먹겠어요.

I'm skipping dinner, but for **a midnight snack**, I'm having a milk shake.

166 밥벌이를 하다(밥값을 하다)

earn one's keep, pay for living

DIALOG

A : 그 집에 공짜로 있나요?

Do you stay at their house free?

B : 아니요, 그 집 아들에게 영어를 가르치고 있으니 **내 밥값은 하고 있지요.**

No, I think I **earn my keep** by teaching their son English.

[Note] keep (사람, 동물의) 생활자료, 음식, 생활비.

167 (이 서점이 내) 밥줄이에요.

This bookstore is my bread and butter.

DIALOG

A : 당신은 다른 직업이 있나요?

Do you have another job?

B : 아니요, 이 서점이 내 **밥줄이에요.**

No, This bookstore is my **bread and butter.**

168 방송으로 사람을 찾다

page

DIALOG

A : 공항에서 어떻게 선생님을 찾을 수 있을까요?

How can I find you at the airport?

B : **이름을 불러 찾아 달라고** 하세요.

Have me **paged**. (혹은 Ask them to **page** me.)

[Note] page 이름을 불러 사람을 찾다

169 방해가 되다

interrupt, be in one's way

DIALOG

A : 제가 **방해가 되지 않을까요**?

Am I **interrupting** anything?

B : 아니요, 전혀.

No, not at all.

170 배달해 주시나요?

Do you have a delivery service?

DIALOG

A : **배달도 해 주시나요?**

Do you have a delivery service?

B : 네, 어디로 **배달해 드릴까요**?

Yes, where do you **want it delivered?**

A : 제 사무실로요.

At my office.

171 벗이 되어 주다

keep someone company

DIALOG

A : 내 **벗이 되어 줄** 애완 동물 한 마리 사고 싶어요.

I'd rather have a pet to **keep me company.**

B : 특별히 생각하고 계시는 것이 있나요?

Anything special in mind?

A : 네, 토끼를 살까 해요.

Yes, a rabbit.

172 변화를 주다

try something different

DIALOG

A : 머리 스타일을 바꿨나요?

Did you change your hairstyle?

B : 예, **변화를 주고 싶었어요.**

Yes, **I wanted to try something different.**

A : 지난번 스타일이 더 좋았는데.

I liked it better the other way.

[Note] 여기서 the other way 대신 before를 사용해도 좋다.

173 보답하다

repay

DIALOG

A : 당신의 호의에 **보답하고** 싶어요.

I'd like to **repay** your hospitality.

B : 친절하신 말씀입니다만 그렇게 할 필요 없어요. 제가 선생님께 해 드린 건 대수롭지 않은 거예요.

That's very kind of you, but you don't need to do that. What I did for you was nothing much.

174 보람이 있다
pay off

DIALOG

A : 저는 정말 열심히 일했습니다.

I really worked hard.

B : 알 수 있어요. 당신이 열심히 일한 **보람이 있어요.**

I can tell. Your hard work has really **paid off.**

175 보인다
show

DIALOG

A : 바지에 커피를 쏟았어요.

I spilled some coffee on my pants.

B : 그런데 안 **보이는데요.**

But it doesn't **show.**

176 보잘 것 없는 존재들
small potatoes

DIALOG

A : 그는 쥐꼬리만큼 돈을 버는 **보잘 것 없는** 자들 중의 하나야.

He's one of those **small potatoes** making chicken feed.

B : 물론 일류 배우가 되는 사람들은 드물지.

Of course, there are very few who make the big time.

[Note] small potatoes 변변치 않은 것(사람들)/chicken feed = small amount of money / big-time 일류의(opp. small-time)

177 보충하다

make up for

DIALOG 1

A : 어제 저녁 데이트 참 재미있었어요.

I had a wonderful time on my date last night.

B : 잘됐군요. 전날 저녁 바람맞은 것에 대한 **보충이 되었겠군요.**

Good. That should **make up for** your being stood up the other night.

[Note] stand someone up (누구를) 바람맞히다

DIALOG 2

A : 이번 주말에 뭐 할 거예요?

What are you going to do this weekend?

B : 뒤떨어진 학과를 **보충하려고 해요.**

Nothing special. I'm going to **catch up on** my school work.

[Note] 그동안 잠을 잘 자지 못해서 잠을 보충하려고 할 때는 "I'm going to catch up on my sleep."

178 (한몫) 보태다

chip in~, contribute, help out

DIALOG 1

A : 한 사람이 지불하기에는 너무 많다고 생각되는군요.

I think it's too much for one person.

B : 모두에게 **한몫씩 보태라고** 부탁합시다.

Why don't we ask everyone to **chip in**?

DIALOG 2

A : 고아들의 선물을 사기 위해 돈을 모으고 있는 것으로 알고 있어요.

I understand you're collecting money for gifts for the orphans.

B : 당신도 **한몫 보태 주시겠어요**?

Would you like to **chip in**, too?

[Note] chip in 대신에 contribute나 help out을 사용해도 좋다. 식사를 한 후에 한 사람이 돈을 내려고 할 때 이쪽에서 "Can I chip in(혹은 contribute 혹은 help out)?"을 사용하면 훌륭하다.

179 본론을 말하다

get to the point

DIALOG

A : 그 전화 무슨 전화였어요?

What was the phone call about?

B : 모르겠어요. **본론은 말하지 않고** 빙빙 돌려서 말하네요.

I don't know. He **never got to the point.** He kept beating around the bush.

[Note] beat around the bush (본론은 말하지 않고) 둘러대다, 간접적으로 말하다.

180 본의가 아니다

I don't mean it.

DIALOG

A : 어떻게 감히 우리 대화를 도청합니까?

How do you eavesdrop on our conversation?

B : **본의가 아니었어요.** 미안합니다. 곧 수화기를 내려놓을게요.

I didn't mean it. I'm sorry. I'll get off the telephone extension right this moment.

181 (그 자리는) 봉급이 많다

The position pays well.

DIALOG

A : 기계공학에 관련된 자리는 매우 중요한 자리야.

A mechanical engineer is a very responsible position.

B : 그리고 **봉급도 많고요.** 하지만 나는 변호사가 되고 싶어요.

And it **pays well**, but I still want to be a lawyer.

182 봐주다

have a heart, have pity

DIALOG

A : 제발 좀 **봐주세요.**

Please **have a heart,** will you?

B : 미안합니다. 예외를 만들 수는 없군요.

I'm sorry. I can't make an exception.

183 부끄럽지도 않니?

Shame on you!

DIALOG

A : 나는 결국 그를 설득시켜서 그 힘든 일을 하게 했어.

I finally talked him into doing the hard work.

B : **부끄럽지도 않니**? 너는 우정을 이용하고 있어.

Shame on you! You're taking advantage of your friendship.

184 부담 갖지 마세요
feel free

DIALOG

A : 언제 만날 수 있을까요?
When can I see you?

B : **부담 갖지 말고** 언제든지 저희 집에 오세요.
Please **feel free** to drop by my house anytime.

185 부담드리고 싶지 않아요
I don't want to impose on you

DIALOG

A : **부담드리고 싶지 않아요.**
I don't want to impose on you.

B : 제발 부담이라 생각지 마세요.
Please don't consider it an imposition.

186 부업으로 일하다
moonlight, wear two hats, have two jobs(혹은 responsibilities)

DIALOG

A : 주말에도 일을 하나요?
Do you work on weekends, too?

B : 네, 식당에서 **부업으로 일해요.**
Yes, **I moonlight** at a restaurant.

[Note] moonlight (동시에) 두 가지 직업으로 일하다. He has two jobs(responsibilities) 또는 He wears two hats.

187 불량품
defective

DIALOG

A : 이것은 **불량품이에요.** 돈으로 반환해 주세요.

This is **defective.** I'd like a refund.

B : 미안하지만 돈으로는 반환이 안 돼요.

I'm afraid we don't give refunds.

[Note] defective 결점, 결함이 있는, 불완전한

188 불청객이 왔어요
I invited myself.

DIALOG

A : **불청객이 왔어요.**

I invited myself.

B : 와 주셔서 고마워요.

Thank you very much for coming.

189 불편을 끼치다
inconvenience

DIALOG

A : **불편을 끼쳐 드리는 것이** 아니기를 바라요.

I hope I'm not **inconveniencing** you.

B : 아니에요. 전혀요.

No, not at all.

190 붙어다니다

stick together

DIALOG

A : 그는 우리하고 가나요?

Is he going with us?

B : 아니요, 그는 그의 친구들하고 가요. 그들은 **늘 붙어다니지요.**

No. He is going with his friends. They **stick together.**

191 비기다(무승부)

a draw, end in a tie(draw)

DIALOG

A : 권투시합이 어떻게 되었어요?

How did the boxing match turn out?

B : **비겼어요(무승부였어요).**

It was a **draw.(It ended in a draw.)**

192 비대한

overweight

DIALOG

A : 그는 정말 **비대하니**?

Is he really **overweight**?

B : 그런 것 같은데요. 수년 동안 점점 비대해지고 있어요.

I'm afraid so. He's been gaining weight for several years.

[Note] gain weight 비대해지다(opp. lose weight)

193 비뚜름하다
crooked

DIALOG

A : 넥타이를 좀 고쳐 매야겠어요. **비뚜름해요.**

You need to adjust your tie. It's **crooked.**

B : 고마워요.

Thank you.

194 비밀로 하다
keep it to yourself

DIALOG

A : 공식적으로 발표할 때까지 **비밀로 해 주세요.**

Please **keep it to yourself**(= Please **keep it secret**) until we announce it officially.

B : 걱정 마세요. 입 다물고 있을 테니까.

Don't worry. My lips are sealed.

[Note] 입을 다물다 seal one's lips, hold one's tongue, shut one's mouth.

195 비밀이다
It's a surprise.

DIALOG

A : 오늘 저녁 요리는 뭐예요?

What's for dinner tonight?

B : **비밀이에요.** 기다려 보세요.

It's a surprise. You'll just have to wait and see.

196 비밀을 누설하다
spill the beans

DIALOG

A : 누가 **비밀을 누설했다고** 의심이 가나요?
Who do you suspect **spilled the beans**?

B : 당신이 모르니 그걸 누가 알겠어요.
Your guess is as good as mine.

[Note] spill the beans = disclose a secret/The trip was supposed to be a secret, but Fred spilled the beans when he mentioned buying plane tickets. 여행은 비밀로 하기로 했는데 프레드가 비행기표 사는 이야기를 했을 때 비밀이 탄로나 버렸다.

197 비번이다
be off

DIALOG

A : 내일 오후 제가 뵈러 가도 될까요?
Can I come in to see you tomorrow afternoon?

B : 내일 제가 **비번입니다.**
I'm going to **be off** tomorrow.

198 비슷하다
identical, be like

DIALOG

A : 당신 글씨체가 저와 **비슷하군요.**
Your handwriting **is** just **like** mine.

B : 네, **꼭 같군요.**
Yes. They're **identical.**

199 비싸다
cost a fortune

DIALOG

A : 그 드레스 정말 잘 어울려요. 그걸 사시겠어요?

That dress really looks nice on you. Are you going to buy it?

B : 아니요. 그걸 살 여유가 없어요. 너무 **비싸요.**

No. I can't afford it. It **costs a fortune.**

[Note] "너무 비싸다"를 too expensive라고 해도 좋다. "값이 터무니없이 비싸다"는 The price is outrageous(혹은 ridiculous)라고 하면 된다.

200 비위를 맞추다
please

DIALOG

A : 남편은 음식에 까다로운가요?

Is your husband fussy about his food?

B : 아니요. **비위 맞추기** 쉬운 사람이에요. 제가 한 요리를 좋아하거든요.

No. He's very easy **to please**. He likes my cooking.

[Note] "음식에 까다롭다"는 be finicky about food라고도 많이 쓴다. "비위를 맞추어 주는, 아첨하는"은 flattering이다. You're very flattering.

201 빈둥빈둥 놀다
goof off, fool around, idle away

DIALOG 1

A : 공부하고 있니, **놀고 있니**?

Are you studying or **goofing off**?

B : 아빠, 미안해요. 공부할게요.

Sorry, Dad. I'll study.

DIALOG 2

A : 지금 **빈둥빈둥 놀** 시간이 아니야.

This is no time for us to **fool around.**

B : 맞아. 일을 시작하자.

You're right. Let's get back to work.

202 빌려준 것(빌린 것)

a loan

DIALOG 1

A : 이게 당신 차인가요?

Is this your car?

B : 아니요. 친구한테서 **빌린 거예요.**

No. It's just a **loan** from my friend.

DIALOG 2

A : 저한테 가지라고 주신 줄 알았어요.

I thought you gave it to me to keep.

B : 그냥 **빌려 드린 거예요.** 도로 주셔야 해요.

It was just a **loan**. I want it back.

203 빨래를 빨다

do the washing(laundry)

DIALOG 1

A : 언제 **빨래를 하나요**?

When do you **do the washing(laundry)**?

B : 매주 금요일마다요.

Every Friday.

DIALOG 2

A : 이 옷 물로 **빨아도 될까요**?

Is this dress **washable**?

B : 아니요, 드라이 크리닝해야 해요.

No, it should be dry cleaned.

A : **빨면 색깔이 변할까요**?

Does it **lose its color in the wash**?

B : 아니요, 걱정하실 필요 없어요

No, you don't have to worry about that.

[Note] "이것은 빨면 준다." This shrinks in the wash. "빨아도 줄지 않는다. 잉크 얼룩은 빨아도 지지 않는다." This is shrinkproof. The ink stain will not come out.

204 뼈빠지게 일하다
work one's head (tail) off

DIALOG

A : **뼈빠지게 일하고** 있어요.

I've been **working my head off.**(= I've been **working my fingers to the bone.**)

B : 기진맥진하시겠군요.

You must be exhausted.

[Note] work one's fingers to the bone. 몸을 아끼지 않고 일하다.

사

205 사고를 당하다

be in an accident

DIALOG

A : 그는 오늘 아침 **교통사고를 당했어요.**

He **was in a traffic accident** this morning.

B : 오, 저런. 지금은 괜찮아요?

Oh, my goodness. Is he all right now?

206 사과할 일이 있다

owe an apology

DIALOG

A : 내가 자네에게 **사과할 일이 있네.**

I **owe** you **an apology.**

B : 무엇 때문에?

What for?

A : 내가 싸움을 시작한 것 같아.

I think I started the fight.

B : 잊어버려! 지나간 일은 지나간 일로 덮어두세.

Forget it! Let bygones be bygones.

[Note] Let bygones be bygones. 과거는 잊어버리자(Let the past be forgotten).

207 사교성이 있다

outgoing

DIALOG

A : 그는 **사교성이 많은** 사람인가?

Is he **outgoing**?

B : 아니요, 수줍음이 많은 편이지요.

No, he's rather shy.

208 사랑에 홀딱 빠져 있다

be head over heels in love

DIALOG

A : 그들은 서로 어떻게 느끼고 있나요?

How do they feel about each other?

B : 그들은 **사랑에 홀딱 빠져 있어요.**

They're **head over heels in love.**

[Note] head over heels 완전히, 열렬히(completely, enthusiastically)

209 사방으로 뿔뿔이 흩어져 있다

scattered all over

DIALOG

A : 옛 친구들과는 전혀 연락이 닿지 않아요.

I've been completely out of touch with my old friends.

B : 그래요, 사람들이 **뿔뿔이 흩어져 있을 때** 연락을 계속한다는 것은 어려운 일이지요.

Yes, it's hard to keep contact when people **scattered all over.**

210 (남의) 사생활에 너무 파고들다

get too personal

DIALOG

A : 부인과 이혼할 거라는 소문이 있던데 사실이에요?

There's a rumor going around that you're getting a divorce. Is it true?

B : **남의 사생활을 너무 파고드는 것** 같군요.

I'm afraid you're **getting too personal.**

211 사직하다(사표를 내다)

resign from~

DIALOG

A : 그는 회사에 **사표를 냈나요**?

Did he **resign from** that company?

B : 아니요, 해고당했어요.

No, he was fired.

212 사이좋게 지내다

hit it off

DIALOG

A : 패티에게서 거의 3주째 소식이 없어요.

I haven't heard from Patti in almost three weeks.

B : 그래요? 당신이 생각하는 것만큼 **사이좋게 지내지** 않았던 모양이지요.

Really? Maybe you didn't **hit it off** as well as you thought.

[Note] hit it off = get along well with each other/We hit it off immediately with the new neighbors. 우리는 새 이웃과 곧 사이좋게 지냈다. She and her brother have never really hit it off. 그녀와 그녀의 오빠는 정말 사이 좋게 지내본 적이 없다.

213 사진이 잘 나오다

take good pictures, photograph well
be photogenic, have a photogenic face

DIALOG

A : 너는 **사진이 잘 나온 거야**, 사진이 잘 받는 얼굴인데.

You must **take** very **good pictures**, you **have a** very **photogenic face**.

B : 그렇게 생각하세요? **저는 사진이 잘 안 받는다고 생각하는데요.**

Do you think so? **I don't think I photograph very well.**

214 사진이 잘 나왔다

pictures turn out all right

DIALOG

A : 오늘 사진을 찾을 수 있을까요?

Can I pick up my pictures today?

B : 잠깐만요, 한번 알아보고요. 네, 준비가 다 됐군요.

Just a moment, I'll check. Yes, they're ready to go.

A : **잘 나왔어요**?

Did they **turn out all right**?

215 사진을 확대하다

blow up

DIALOG

A : 이 사진을 **확대해 주세요.**

I **want** a **blow up** of this picture.(= I want this picture blown up.)

B : 크기는 얼마로 할까요?

All right. What size would you like?

A : 가로 7인치 세로 11인치.

Seven by eleven.

B : 몇 장 해 드릴까요?

How many copies do you need?

[Note] blow up 확대하다(enlarge) / blow-up 확대된 사진 또는 그림

216 (할 일이) 산더미처럼 쌓인

be up to one's ears in~, be behind in~

DIALOG

A : 오늘 저녁 식사에 초대하고 싶은데요.

I would like to invite you to dinner tonight.

B : 정말 가고 싶지만 안되겠어요. 할 일이 **산더미처럼 쌓여 있어요.**

I'd love to come but I can't. **I'm up to my ears in work.**(I'm behind in work.)

217 산책에 데리고 가다

walk an animal

DIALOG

A : 왜 비가 오는데 나가나요?

Why are you going out in the rain?

B : 개를 산책시켜야 해요.

I have to **walk my dog.**

218 살다 보니 별일 다 보겠군

Now I've seen everything!

DIALOG 1

A : 아이구! 비키니 수영복 입은 저 여자 좀 봐요.

Good grief! Look at that woman in the bikini!

B : 오래 살다보니 별일 다 보겠군!

Now I've seen everything!

219 살아가다

support oneself

DIALOG

A : 작년 9월부터 실직 상태인데 아직도 일자리를 구하지 못했어요.

I've been out of a job since September last year, and I haven't landed one yet.

B : 어떻게 **살아가나요?**

How are you **supporting yourself?**

A : 실직 수당을 받고 있지요.

I'm getting unemployment benefits.

220 살이 찌다

put on weight

DIALOG

A : 당신 생각에 제가 헬스클럽에 가입해야 될 것 같나요?

Do you think I should join a health club.

B : 그래요. 운동이 도움이 될 거예요. 당신은 **살이 찌고 있어요.**

Yes. Exercise would do you good. You're **putting on a few pounds.**

[Note] "You're getting fat." 즉 "당신은 뚱뚱해져 간다"라고 표현하면 정중하지 못하니 사용하지 않는 것이 좋다.

221 살피다

keep an eye on

DIALOG

A : 그를 잘 **살펴봐**. 다시 잠들지 모르니까.

Keep an eye on him. He might fall asleep again.

B : 걱정 마세요. 그런 일이 다시는 발생하지 않도록 하지요.

Don't worry. I won't let it happen again.

222 상심하지 마세요

Don't take it too hard, Don't be broken-hearted.

DIALOG

A : 나는 그의 잔소리에 진저리가 나. 더 이상 그와 일할 기분이 안 나.

I'm sick and tired of his constant nagging. I don't feel like working with him any more.

B : **너무 상심하지 마세요.** 그는 늘 잔소리꾼이니까요.

Don't take it too hard. He's always been a nagger(chatterbox).

[Note] be sick and tired 진저리나다, 구역질나다/feel like ~ing ~하고 싶은 기분이다, ~하고 싶은 마음이 내키다.

223 새벽 1시, 2시경

during the wee hours

DIALOG

A : 보통 몇 시에 주무세요?

What time do you go to bed normally?

B : **새벽 1시, 2시경**에 잡니다. 12시 전에 취침하는 일은 없어요.

I retire **during the wee hours**, and never before midnight.

[Note] retire 은퇴하다, 후퇴하다, 잠자리에 들다

224 새치기하다

cut in ahead of other people

DIALOG

A : 줄이 너무 길군요.

It's too long a line.

B : 그렇지만 **새치기는** 안돼요. 줄을 서야 해요.

You shouldn't **cut in ahead of other people**. You must get in line.

225 생각나는 대로 하다

play it by ear

DIALOG

A : 휴가 계획을 세웠나요?

Have you made definite plans for your vacation?

B : 아니요, **생각나는 대로** 할 예정이에요.

No, I'll just **play it by ear**.

[Note] play it by ear 생각나는 대로 하다, 바람부는 대로 하다(어떤 계획을 미리 세우지 않고)

226 생각이 날 것이다

It'll come to you.

DIALOG

A : 그의 이름이 뭐지요?

What's his name?

B : 혀끝에서 뱅뱅 도는데… 생각이 안 나는군요.

It's on the tip of my tongue, but I can't remember.

A : 괜찮아요. **생각이 날 거예요.**

That's OK. **It'll come to you.**

[Note] be on the tip of one's tongue 혀끝에 뱅뱅 돌다, 생각이 날 듯 날 듯하다.

227 생각해 보니

Come to think of it

DIALOG

A : 쇼핑 가는데 같이 가요.

Why don't you join us? We're going shopping.

B : **생각해 보니** 물건을 좀 사야겠 어요. 좋아요.

Come to think of it, I do need some things. All right.

228 (다시) 생각해 보다

have second thoughts

DIALOG

A : 그 일자리를 갖기 전에 **다시 생각해 보지** 않았나요?

Didn't you **have second thoughts** before you took the job?

B : 아니요, 괜찮을 거라고 생각했지요.

No, not really. I thought it would be all right.

229 (~에 대해 많이) 생각하다

give a lot of thought

DIALOG

A : 여자 친구와 헤어지기로 결심했어요.

I made up my mind to split up with my girl friend.

B : 정말? 참 안됐군. 그러기 전에 다시 한번 생각해 봐요.

Really? That's too bad. Think twice before you do it.

A : 그것에 대해 많이 **생각해 봤어요.**

I've **given** it a lot of **thought.**

[Note] split up 쪼개다, 분열시키다(하다), 헤어지다(divide, separate, get a divorce)

230 (오늘은 매우) 생산적이었어

Today was very productive.

DIALOG

A : 오늘 어땠어요?

How was today?

B : 오늘은 매우 **생산적이었어요.**(한 일이 많았어요)

Today was very **productive.**

231 서류를 제출하다

send in forms

DIALOG

A : 벌써 장학금을 신청했나요?

Have you applied for your scholarship?

B : 네, 모든 **서류를 다 제출했어요.**

Yes, **I've sent in all the forms.**

232 서슴지 말고 ~하세요

Be my guest, Feel free

DIALOG

A : 볼펜 좀 빌릴까요?

May I borrow your ball point pen, please

B : **서슴지 말고 사용하세요.**

Be my guest.(또는 **Feel free.**)

DIALOG 2

A : 정말로 제가 여기에 앉아도 괜찮을까요?

Are you sure it's all right if I sit here?

B : 물론이죠, **어서요.**(**서슴지 말고 앉으세요**)

Sure, **be my guest.**

233 선착순이다

First come, first served.

DIALOG

A : 컴퓨터를 예약해야 하나요?

Do you have to reserve a computer?

B : 아니요, **선착순이에요.**

No, it's on a **first-come, first-served** basis.

234 (요리가) 설익다

undercooked, underdone

DIALOG

A : 파티 음식은 어땠나요?

How was the food at the party?

B : 형편없었어요. 모든 것이 **너무 익혔거나 덜 익혔어요.**

Terrible! Everything was either **overcooked or undercooked.**

235 성과가 있다(보람이 있다)

pay off

DIALOG 1

A : 그는 고등학교를 우등으로 졸업했어요.

He graduated from high school with honors.

B : 열심히 공부한 **성과가 있었군요.**

His hard work has **paid off.**

DIALOG 2

A : 그는 테니스 시합에서 우승했어요.

He won the first prize in the tennis game.

B : 레슨 받은 것이 **성과가 있었군.**

Taking lessons has **paid off.**

236 성의만 해도 고마워요

It's the thought that counts.

DIALOG

A : 오, 이런! 이 인형 좀 봐요. 당신 선물로 샀는데 짐꾸러미 속에서 찌그러졌어요.

Oh, my God! Look at this doll. I bought it for your present, but it got all crushed in the baggage.

B : 괜찮아요. **성의만 해도 고마워요.**

That's all right. **It's the thought that counts.**

[Note] crush 찌그러뜨리다, 눌러 부수다

237 성장(盛裝)하다(잘 차려 입다)

be all dressed up

DIALOG

A : 그렇게 **성장한** 특별한 이유라도 있나요?

Do you have any special reason for **being all dressed up**?

B : 네, 오늘 취업 면접이에요.

Yes, I have a job interview today.

238 성질이 급하다

be quick tempered

DIALOG

A : 그에게 따끔하게 한마디 해야겠어.

I'm going to give him a piece of my mind.

B : **너무 성질 급하게 굴지 마세요.**

Don't be so quick tempered.

DIALOG 2

A : 그는 화를 잘 내요, 그렇지 않아요?

He loses his temper easily, doesn't he?

B : 네. 그는 **성질이 매우 급해요.**

Yes. He's very **quick tempered.**

[Note] lose one's temper 화내다(get angry)/give someone a piece of one's mind "자기의 생각하는 바를 정확하게 말하다"에서 "따끔하게 한마디 하다."

239 세월이 잘 간다(더디게 간다)

How time flies! (Time is really dragging!)

DIALOG

A : **세월이 잘 가네**요. 크리스마스가 바로 눈앞에 다가왔어요.

How time flies! Christmas is just around the corner.

B : 저에겐 세월이 정말 **더디게 가는데요.**

Time is really dragging for me.

240 소란을 피우다

make a scene

DIALOG

A : 그것에 대해 그에게 따끔하게 한마디 하려고요.

I'm going to give him a piece of my mind about that.

B : **소란 피우지 마**시고 그냥 내버려 두세요.

Don't **make a scene**. Why don't you let it go?

241 소망대로 해 줄게요

Your wish is my command.

DIALOG

A : 당신이 저에게 해 주시기를 바라는 것이 하나 더 있어요.

There is just one more thing I'd like you to do.

B : 당신의 **소망대로 해 드리지요.**(분부대로 하겠습니다.)

Your wish is my command!

242 소식을 알리다

keep a person informed(= keep in touch with~)

DIALOG 1

A : 근래 그의 소식을 들었나요?

Have you heard from him lately?

B : 아니요, 거의 1년간 **소식이 끊어졌어요.**

No, we've been out of touch for almost a year.

DIALOG 2

A : 당신이 여행하는 동안 소식을 듣기 바랍니다.

We'd better hear from you during your trip.

B : 네, 틀림없이 소식을 계속 알려 드릴게요.

Yes, sir. I'll be sure to **keep you informed**.

[Note] 멀리 가 있는 동안에도 계속 연락 바라네. Be sure to keep in touch with me while you are away.

243 소중하다

mean a lot

DIALOG

A : 여행에서 가지고 온 기념품들 모두 간직할 거니?

Are you going to keep all these souvenirs from your trip?

B : 네. 버리지 마세요. 그것들은 저에게 아주 **소중해요.**

Oh, yes. Never throw them out. They **mean a lot** to me.

[Note] 그는 나에게 아주 소중한 분이에요. He means the world to me.

244 (가장) 소중한 것을 바치다

give one's eyeteeth

DIALOG

A : 나는 그 자리를 포기하려고 해

I'm going to give up the position.

B : 내가 그것을 얻을 수 있다면 **나의 가장 소중한 것도 바치겠다.**

I'd **give my eyeteeth** to have it.

[Note] eyetooth (특히 위턱의) 송곳니(그 위치가 눈 아래 있기 때문에)/give one's

eyeteeth 자기의 소중한 것을 바치다(자기가 원하는 물건이나 직장 등과 교환으로)/She would give her eyeteeth for that job. 그녀는 그 일자리를 얻을 수만 있다면 어떤 대가라도 치를 것이다.

245 소중히 간직하다
treasure

DIALOG

A : 그걸 어떻게 하려고 하니?
What are you going to do with it?

B : 나는 이것을 여생 동안 **소중히 간직할 거예요.**
I'll **treasure** this for the rest of my life.

246 소지품
one's belongings

DIALOG 1

A : 그에게 자기 **소지**품을 치우도록 가르쳐야 해요.
You should teach him to pick up his **belongings**.

B : 네, 나이가 좀 들면 그러지요. 지금은 너무 어려요.
Yes, I will when he's a little older. He's too young.

247 속이 좋지 않다
My stomach is upset.

DIALOG

A : 그 샐러드를 먹지 않았어야 했는데.
I don't think we should have eaten that salad.

B : 왜요? **속이 좋지 않나요?**
Why, is **your stomach upset**?

248 손가락 마디를 딱딱 소리내다

crack one's knuckles

DIALOG

A : 제발 그 **손가락 마디를 딱딱 하고 소리 내지 마세요**. 그 소리 못 듣겠어요.

Please stop **cracking your knuckles**. It sounds awful!

B : 미안해요. 저는 제가 그러고 있는 것조차 몰랐어요. 습관인가 봐요.

I'm sorry, I didn't even realize I was doing it. It's force of habit.

[Note] force of habit 습관적인 것

249 손이 많이 간다

require a lot of work

DIALOG

A : 이 정원은 원예 솜씨나 우연의 결과가 아니에요.

This garden is not the result of a green thumb or luck.

B : 그렇지 않아요?

It isn't?

A : 제 말을 믿으세요. 정원 가꾼다는 것은 **손이 많이 가요.**

Take my word for it, gardening **requires a lot of work.**

250 손보다(고치다)

work on

DIALOG

A : 그 도구들을 들고 어딜 가나요?

Where are you going with all those tools?

B : 차고에 가요. 잠깐 차에 **손볼 것이** 있어서요.

To the garage. I'm going to **work on** the car for a while.

251 손이 모자라다
short-handed

DIALOG 1
A : 오늘 오후에 휴가를 얻을 수 있을까요?
Can I take the afternoon off?

B : 도저히 불가능해요. 지금도 **손이 모자라는데요.**
It's absolutely out of the question. We're **short-handed** as it is.

DIALOG 2
A : 고객이 너무 많군요.
You have too many customers.

B : **손이 모자랄 뿐이에요.**
We're just **short-handed.**

252 손해 보다
lose money

DIALOG
A : 정말 염가로 봉사하고 있어요. 면도, 이발, 머리감기, 손톱 손질, 구두닦이 모두를 10달러에 해 드립니다.
I'm offering a real bargain; a shave, haircut, shampoo, manicure, shoe shine, the works for ten dollars.

B : 그러면 **손해보지 않나요?**
Won't you **lose money** on that?

253 수첩에 적어 두다
mark on one's calendar

DIALOG

A : 내일 김포공항까지 차가 꼭 필요한데 도와줄 수 있나요?

Tomorrow we need a ride to Kimpo Airport very badly. Are you sure you'll be able to help out?

B : 물론이죠. 잊지 않도록 **수첩에 적어 놓겠어요.**

Sure. I'll **mark** it **on my calendar** so I don't forget.

[Note] calendar '연중행사표, 예정표'에서 '수첩'이라 해도 좋다.

254 수포로 돌아가다

be down the tube, come to nothing(또는 naught)

DIALOG

A : 단서를 잘못 잡아 일주일간의 수사가 **수포로 돌아갔어요.**

We've followed a wrong clue and a whole week's investigation **is down the tube.**

B : 참 안됐군요.

That's too bad.

255 수화기를 내려놓다

take the phone off the hook

DIALOG

A : 전화가 많이 와서 대화에 방해되니 **수화기를 내려놓으세요.**

I don't want our conversation to be interrupted by phone calls. Please **take the phone off the hook.**

B : 네, 좋은 생각이에요. 대화가 끝난 다음 도로 올려놓지요.

Yes, it's a good idea. We can put it back on the hook after our conversation.

256 숨을 돌리다
catch one's breath

DIALOG 1
A : 당신 정말 몹시 지친 것 같군요.
You really look exhausted!

B : 그래요. **숨 좀 돌려야겠어요.**
I am. Let me **catch my breath.**

DIALOG 2
A : 막 테니스가 끝났어요.
I just finished playing tennis.

B : 앉아서 **숨 좀 돌리시죠.**
Sit down and **catch your breath.**

257 쉬는 날
one's day off

DIALOG
A : 언제 쇼핑 갈 거예요?
When do you plan to go shopping?

B : **쉬는 날** 갈까 해요.
I'm going shopping **on my day off.**

258 며칠 쉬다
have a couple of days off

DIALOG
A : 저는 **며칠간 쉬었으면** 좋겠어요.
I'd like to **have a couple of days off.**

B : 기록을 보니 당신은 하루도 쉴 날이 없어요.

According to my records, you have none coming.

259 쉬어 가며 천천히 하다

take it easy

DIALOG

A : 너무 무리하지 마세요. **쉬어 가면서 천천히 해요.**

You shouldn't be pushing yourself so hard; **take it easy.**

B : 맞는 말씀이에요.

You're right.

260 스케줄이 어때요?

What is on your schedule(agenda)?

DIALOG 1

A : 오늘 저녁 **스케줄이 어때요?**

What is on your agenda (schedule) tonight?

B : 특별한 것 없어요.

Nothing special.

DIALOG 2

A : 우리가 11시 30분에 만나기로 했는데, 예기치 않은 일이 생겨 3시로 바꿀 수 있을까요?

I know we're supposed to meet at 11:30, but something came up unexpectedly. Would you mind changing it to 3:00?

B : 괜찮아요, **제 스케줄은 바꿀 수 있어요. 당신 스케줄대로 하세요.**

No, not at all. **My schedule is flexible, so suit yours, please.**

[Note] 스케줄이 바쁘다. I have a heavy schedule.

261 스트레스를 해소하다
get rid of stress

DIALOG

A : 규칙적으로 스트레스를 멀리하는 것이 필요해요.
It is necessary for us to get away from stress regularly.

B : 그래요. **스트레스 해소**에는 테니스가 도움이 되지요.
You're right. Tennis helps you to **get rid of your stress**.

262 습관을 들이다
make a habit of~

DIALOG

A : 한 달에 한두 번 늦는 것은 괜찮아요.
It's all right if you're late once or twice a month.

B : 그렇지만 그것이 **습관이 되어서는 안 돼요**, 알았어요?
But don't **make a habit of it**, right?

263 (나쁜) 습관을 고치다
break a bad habit

DIALOG 1

A : 나는 자네가 담배를 끊을 거라고 생각했지.
I thought you were going to quit smoking

B : 그 **습관을 고칠 수가** 없어요. 인이 박혔어요.
I can't **break the habit**, I'm addicted to nicotine.

[Note] be addicted to~ ~에 빠져 있다, ~에 몰두하다

DIALOG 2

A : 왜 늘 헛기침을 하지요?

Why do you clear your throat all the time?

B : 습관이에요.

It's force of habit.

A : **고치시지요.**

I wish you'd **break it.**

[Note] clear one's throat (말, 노래를 시작하기 전에) 헛기침을 하다

264 승진하다

get a promotion

DIALOG

A : 무슨 일이에요? 무슨 신나는 일이라도 있나요?

What's up? Anything exciting?

B : 별로요, 제가 **승진했어요.**

Nothing much. But I **got a promotion.**

265 시간 가는 줄 모르다

lose track of the time

DIALOG

A : 벌써 12시예요? 이야기하느라고 정말 **시간 가는 줄 몰랐네요.**

It's 12 o'clock already? I have **lost track of the time** talking with you.

B : 커피 한잔 할 시간 있어요?

Do you have time for a cup of coffee?

A : 없을 것 같군요. 가봐야겠어요.

I'm afraid not. I must be going.

266 시간에 겨우 대어 오다

make it by the skin of one's teeth, It's about time.

DIALOG 1

A : 시간에 겨우 대어 왔군요. 당신을 거의 포기했었는데.

It's about time. We almost gave up on you.

B : 미안해요. 타이어가 펑크났어요.

I'm sorry. I had a flat tire.

DIALOG 2

A : 아침 식사 시간에 늦었어요?

Am I late for breakfast?

B : **아슬아슬하게 대어 왔어요.**

You just made it by the skin of your teeth.

[Note] 그는 기차 시간에 겨우 대어 왔다.

He just made the train by the skin of his teeth.

267 시간을 내다

spare some time

DIALOG 1

A : 오늘 오전 시간 **좀 내주시겠어요**? 테니스 시합에 관해 상의해야 하는데.

Can you **spare some time** this morning?

We need to discuss our tennis game.

B : 내일이 어때요? 오늘은 시간을 낼 수가 없어요.

How about tomorrow? I can't spare the time today.

DIALOG 2

A : 주말에 **시간 좀 내줄 수** 있어요? 테니스를 같이 치고 싶어요.

Could you **spare some time** on the weekend?

I want to play tennis with you.

B : 그럼요, 저는 요즘 시간이 너무 많아 주체 못하고 있어요.

Sure. Time hangs heavy on my hands.

[Note] 근래 저는 직업이 없어, 시간이 남아 주체 못하고 있어요.

Recently I don't have a job, so time hangs heavy on my hands.

268 시간을 때우다

kill time

DIALOG

A : 지금 바쁘세요?

Are you busy now?

B : 아니요, **시간을 때우고** 있는 중이에요.

No, I'm just **killing time**.

269 시간을 너무 빼앗다

take up too much of one's time

DIALOG

A : 커피나 한잔 하고 더 있다 가세요.

Why don't you stay longer for a cup of coffee?

B : 글쎄요, 당신 **시간을 너무 많이 빼앗고 싶지 않군요.**

Well, I don't want to **take up too much of your time.**

270 (빈) 시간이 있다

have an opening

DIALOG 1

A : 오늘 오후 늦게 만날 약속을 할 수 있을까요?
Can I make an appointment for later today?

B : 물론이죠, 2시와 4시 사이에 **빈 시간이 있어요.**
Sure. We **have an opening** between 2 and 4.

A : 그러면 2시 30분으로 해 주세요.
Make it 2:30, then.

B : 좋아요, 그런데 2시 20분이나 2시 40분, 즉 10분의 여유는 주세요.
OK, give or take 10 minutes.

[Note] opening (지위 따위의) 공석, (취직, 돈벌이의) 자리, 기회(opportunity)/give or take 시간을 약속할 때 몇 분은 빨리 갈 수도 있고 또 반대로 늦게 갈 수도 있다. 그 때 몇 분의 여유는 감안해 달라는 뜻으로 쓴다.

DIALOG 2

A : 이번 수요일에 **빈 시간이 없어요.**
I don't have any **openings** this Wednesday.

B : 약속 시간들 사이에 하나 끼어 줄 수 없나요?
Can't you squeeze me in between appointments?

[Note] squeeze 쑤셔 (틀어) 넣다

271 (그가) 시간이 있는지 없는지
if he is available

DIALOG

A : 김 교수님을 만나뵐 약속을 하고 싶은데요.
I'd like to make an appointment to see Professor Kim.

B : 끊지 말고 기다리세요. **그분 시간이 있는지 없는지 알아볼게요.**
누가 전화했다고 할까요?

Hold on, please. I'll see if he's available. Who shall I tell him is calling?

[Note] make an appointment 약속하다/Who is calling? 전화한 분은 누구신가요?

272 시계 방향으로 달리다
run clockwise

DIALOG

A : 모든 사람들이 같은 **시계 방향으로 달리고 있군요.**

Every runner is **running** in the same direction **clockwise.**

B : 네, 월요일, 수요일, 금요일은 시계 방향으로, 화요일, 목요일, 토요일, 일요일은 시계 반대 방향으로 달리지요.

Yes, all runners will **run clockwise** on Monday, Wednesday and Friday, and **counter-clockwise** on Tuesday, Thursday, Saturday and Sunday.

273 시대에 뒤떨어진
behind the times

DIALOG

A : 그는 상대편을 **시대에 뒤떨어지고** 한물갔다고 부르더군.

He called his opponent "**behind the times**" and "over the hill."

B : 그는 상대방의 나이가 많은 것을 이용하고 있지요.

He was trying to take advantage of his challenger's age.

274 (일에) 시달리다
be under pressure at work

DIALOG

A : 나는 일에 **시달리고 있어요.** 한 사람 일이 너무 많아요.

I'm **under a lot of pressure at work.** There's just too much work for one person.

B : 그 시달림에서 곧 벗어나기를 바라요.

I hope **the pressure is off** you soon.

275 시설이 좋다

have fine accommodations

DIALOG

A : 힐튼 호텔 어때요?

How about the Hilton Hotel?

B : **훌륭한 시설을 갖추고 있습니다만** 좀 비싸요.

It has fine accommodations, but it's a little expensive.

276 시시한 것들(보잘것없는 것들)

trinket, trifle

DIALOG

A : 이것들은 가치가 있나요?

Is any of this stuff valuable?

B : 아니요, 그저 **시시한 것들이에요.**

No, they're all just **trinkets.**

277 시야를 막다

block one's view

DIALOG

A : 여기에 서도 될까요?

May I stand here?

B : 네, 하지만 왼쪽으로 약간 비켜 서 주세요. 그러면 **시야를 막지 않거든요.**

Yes, but move to the left a little, so you don't **block my view.**

278 시치미 떼다

play innocent with

DIALOG

A : 나한테 **시치미 떼지 마.** 그 사실을 다 알고 있으니까.

Don't **play innocent with** me. I know the fact.

B : 나는 정말 몰라요.

I really don't know the fact.

279 시험 어떻게 치렀니?

How did your test go?

How did you do on your test?

DIALOG

A : **시험 어떻게 치렀니?**

How did your test go?(혹은 **How did you do on your test?**)

B : 100점 받았어요. 틀린 것은 하나도 없어요.

I got 100%. I didn't make any mistakes.

280 시험해 보다

give it a try

DIALOG

A : 최근에 문 연 한국 식당을 알고 있는데 한번 **시험해 봅시다.** 제가 살게요.

I know a new Korean restaurant that opened recently. **Let's give it a try.** I'm buying.

B : 좋은 생각이에요.

Sounds great.

281 식사를 더 하다
have some more

DIALOG

A : 이거 정말 맛있네요. **더 먹어도 괜찮을까요?**

This is really delicious. **Do you suppose I can have some more?**

B : 물론이죠. 두 그릇째밖에 안 되는데요.

Sure. That's only **your second helping.**

[Note] helping (음식) 한 사람 몫, 한 그릇/a second helping 두 그릇째

282 식욕이 왕성하다
have a big appetite(have an appetite like a wild animal)

DIALOG

A : 두 어린 아들의 **식욕이 왕성하군요.**

Your two young sons **have appetites like wild animals.**

B : 네, 언젠가는 우리 재산을 다 먹어 치울 겁니다.

Yes, I wouldn't be surprised if one day they ate us out of house and home.

[Note] eat (a person) out of house and home (~의 재산을) 다 먹어 치우다 (없애다)

283 신경을 건드리다
get on one's nerves(= irritate one's nerves)

DIALOG

A : 손가락 마디를 딱딱 하는 것 좀 하지 말게. **내 신경을 건드리는군.**
Don't crack your knuckles. **It's getting on my nerves.**

B : 미안해요. 몰랐어요.
I'm sorry. I didn't know that.

284 (결국) ~신세가 되다
wind up ~ing

DIALOG 1

A : **결국은 주위에 친구가 하나도 없는 신세가 될 거예요.**
You'll wind up having no friends.

B : 누가 걱정한답니까? 그들 없이도 살 수 있어요.
Who cares? I can get by without them.

[Note] get by 쉽게 성공하다, 문제화되지 않다. 용케 헤어나다.

DIALOG 2

A : 너무 속도 내지 마세요, 당신이 **결국 딱지를 떼는 신세가 되는 걸** 원치 않아요.
Don't speed, I don't want you to wind up getting a ticket.

B : 걱정 마세요. 속도 제한보다 5마일 초과해서 달릴 뿐이에요.
Don't worry, I'm only going five miles over the speed limit.

285 신물이 나다
be fed up with(= be sick and tired of~, have had~)

DIALOG

A : 형편없는 식사야! 이젠 기숙사 음식에 **신물이 나.**

What a lousy meal! **I'm fed up with** dorm food.

B : 그 말 잘했어. 나도 **신물이 나.** 더 이상 못 참겠다.

You said it.(혹은 You can say that again.)

I'm sick and tired of it, too. Enough is enough!

C : 나도 **신물이 나.**

I've had it, too.

286 실물이 어떻게 생겼니?

How does he (she) look in real life?

DIALOG

A : 나는 그가 주유소에서 차에 손수 기름을 넣고 있는 걸 보았어요.

I saw him gassing up his car personally at a filling station.

B : 그래? **실물은 어떻든?**

Did you? **How did he look in real life?**

A : 영화에서보다 약간 젊어 보였어요.

He looked a little younger than in the movie.

287 실물이 훨씬 낫다

look much better in real life

DIALOG

A : 이 사진이 잘 안 나왔어. **너는 실물이 훨씬 나아.**

This picture didn't turn out very well. **You look much better in real life.**

B : 칭찬해 줘서 고마워요.

Thanks for the compliment.

288 실언을 하다

put one's foot in it(= put one's foot in one's mouth)

DIALOG 1

A : 그녀가 왜 화났니?

Why is she upset?

B : 그녀의 남편이 머리 스타일이 안 좋다고 했대.

Her husband criticized her hair style.

A : 어머! 그가 **큰 실언을 했구나.**

Wow! He really **put his foot in his mouth.**

DIALOG 2

A : 그의 아버지가 왜 화가 나셨니?

Why is his father so angry?

B : 그가 말대꾸를 했어요.

He talked back to his father.

A : 그가 **큰 실언을 했구나.**

He really **put his foot in it.**

289 (불경기로) 실직하다

be laid off

DIALOG

A : 남편이 불경기로 **실직당했어요.**

My husband **got laid off from his job.**

B : 어떻게 살아가지요?

How are you supporting yourselves?

A : 실직 수당을 받고 있어요.

He's getting unemployment benefits.

290 (너무) 심하게 하다

be too harsh on~

DIALOG

A : 그가 괜찮을까요?

Do you think he'll be all right?

B : 솔직히 말해서 **너무 심하게 했어요.**

Frankly speaking, you **were too harsh on him.**

291 쌀쌀한 태도를 보이다

give one the cold shoulder

DIALOG

A : 너 우울해 보이는데, 무슨 일이니?

You look down. Anything wrong?

B : 요즘 여자 친구가 나에게 **쌀쌀한 태도를 보이고 있어.**

My girl friend has been **giving me the cold shoulder lately.**

A : 너무 상심하지 마. 낙관적인 면을 생각해.

Don't take it too hard. Look on the bright side.

B : 어떤 낙관적인 면을?

What bright side?

A : 데이트할 여자는 그 여자뿐만이 아니란 거지.

There're other fish in the sea.

292 (몸이) 쑤시고 아픈 데 먹을 약

medication for aches and pains

DIALOG

A : 어떻게 오셨나요?

What's the problem?

B : **쑤시고 아픈 데 먹을** 약 좀 주세요.

I need **something**(혹은 **some medication**) **for my aches and pains.**

293 쓰레기 같은(것)

a piece of garbage, trashy, junk

DIALOG 1

A : 내가 좋아하는 음식은 아이스크림과 감자칩이에요.

My favorite foods are ice cream and potato chips.

B : 어떻게 그런 **쓰레기 같은** 것들을 견뎌내나요?

How can your body stand such **junk** food?

DIALOG 2

A : 잘못 생각하지 마.

Don't get the wrong idea.

B : 무엇을?

What?

A : 이 **쓰레기 같은 잡지**는 나를 위한 것이 아니고 내 언니를 위한 거라구. 그녀는 얼빠진 이유로 이 **쓰레기 같은** 것을 좋아해.

I didn't buy this **trashy** magazine for myself, it's for my sister. For some crazy reason, she loves this **junk**.

DIALOG 3

A : 그 영화 정말 좋았어요. 그렇게 생각지 않나요?

The movie was pretty good, don't you think so?

B : 농담이겠지요. 그것은 **쓰레기 같은** 엉터리 작품이에요.

You're kidding. It was **a piece of garbage**.

아

294 (내가) 아는 바로는 아무 일이 없다

Nothing that I know of.

DIALOG

A : 그녀에게 무슨 일이 있나요? 무엇인가에 화가 난 것 같아요.

What's the matter with her? She seems angry about something.

B : **내가 아는 바로는 아무 일 없어요.**

Nothing that I know of.

295 아슬아슬하다(위험하다)

That was a close call, That was a narrow escape.

DIALOG

A : 저 차가 하마터면 길 건너는 사람을 칠 뻔했어. 야, **아슬아슬했어.**

That crazy car almost ran over a man crossing the street. Boy, **that was a close call**!(or **that was close**!)

B : 그래요, 정말 **아슬아슬했어요.**

Yeah, **that** really **was a narrow escape.**

[Note] a close call = a close shave = a narrow escape 아슬아슬하게 피하는 것

296 (맛이) 오십 가지나 있다

have 50 flavors

DIALOG

A : 어떤 아이스크림이 있어요?

What kind(of ice-cream) do you have?

B : **오십 가지나 있습니다.**

We have 50 flavors.

A : 그럼 초콜릿으로 주세요.

Okay, I'll take chocolate.

297 아직 멀었다

have a long way to go

DIALOG

A : 언제 졸업해요?

How soon do you graduate?

B : 학위를 마치려면 **아직 멀었어요.**

I still **have a long way to go** to finish my degree.

298 아파서 결근한다고 알리다

call in sick

DIALOG 1

A : 배가 몹시 아파요.

I have a terrible stomachache.

B : **아파서 결근한다고** 알리지 그래요?

Why don't you **call in sick**?

DIALOG 2

A : 오늘은 일할 기분이 안 나는데, 아파서 못 간다고 알려야겠어요.

I don't feel like working today. I'm going to **call in sick.**

B : 아프다고요?

Are you sick?

A : 아니요, 다만 하루 쉬고 싶어요. 내가 없이도 해 나가거든요.

No, I just want to have a day off. They can manage without me.

299 입에서 악취가 나다
have bad breath

DIALOG

A : 뭘 먹었니?

What have you been eating?

B : 왜요?

Why?

A : **입에서 악취가 나**. 제발 얼굴을 돌려.

You have bad breath! Face the other way, please!

[Note] 입에서 담배 냄새가 나다. Her breath smells of cigarette smoke.
파슬리를 먹으면 입에서 악취가 없어진다. Parsley takes away bad breath.

300 악화되다
change for the worse

DIALOG

A : 부인의 병세가 **악화되지** 않기를 바랍니다.

I hope your wife improves and doesn't have **a change for the worse**.

B : 염려해 주셔서 감사합니다.

Thank you for your concern.

301 (정말) 안됐군요
That's a shame!

DIALOG 1

A : 너희들과 볼링을 치러 갈 수 없겠구나.

I can't go bowling with you guys.

B : **정말 안됐군요.** 선생님 없이는 재미가 없어요.

That's a shame! It's no fun without you.

DIALOG 2

A : 그가 사고를 당했다니 **참 안됐어요.**

It's a shame that he had an accident.

B : 크게 다치지는 않았어요.

He wasn't badly hurt.

302 안색도 변하지 않는다

keep a straight face

DIALOG

A : 그는 우리에게 터무니없는(어리석은) 이야기를 했어요.

He told us a very ridiculous story.

B : 알아요. **안색도 변하지 않고** 태연한 척하기란 아주 힘들었어요.

I know. I could hardly **keep a straight face.**

303 안전벨트를 착용하다

buckle up

DIALOG

A : **안전벨트를 착용해야 해요.**

You should buckle up.

B : 저는 항상 차를 타자마자 해요.

I always do as soon as I get in the car.

[Note] buckle up 조임쇠로 죄다.

304 (하는 일 없이) 앉아 있다

be sitting around

DIALOG 1

A : 제가 방해가 되나요?

Am I interrupting you?

B : 아니요, **하는 일 없이 앉아 있을 뿐이에요.**

No, **I'm just sitting around.**

DIALOG 2

A : 설거지 하는 것 좀 도와주겠니?

Will you help me do the dishes?

B : 물론이죠, **하는 일 없이 앉아 있을 뿐인데요.**

Sure, **I'm just sitting around.**

[Note] do the dishes 접시 닦기하다, 설거지하다

305 (내가) 알기에는 ~아니다

not that I know of

DIALOG

A : 그 컴퓨터에 무슨 이상이 있나요?

Is there something wrong with the computer?

B : **내가 알기에는그렇지 않은데요.**

Not that I know of.(= Not so far as I know.)

306 (다른 데) 알아보다

get a second opiniorn

DIALOG

A : 제 생각에는 너무 비싼 것 같군요.

I think it's too expensive.

B : **다른 데 좀 알아보지요.**

Why don't you **get a second opinion?**(Why don't you **shop around**?)

307 알아서 하다(당신에게 달려 있다)

It's up to you.

DIALOG 1

A : 그 파티에 친구들 몇 명 데리고 가도 괜찮을까요?

May I bring some friends to the party?

B : 물론이죠. **알아서 하세요.**

Sure. **It's up to you.**

DIALOG 2

A : 브라운색 신발을 살까, 검정색 신발을 살까?

Should I buy the brown shoes or the black shoes?

B : **알아서 하세요.**

It's up to you.

308 애타 죽겠다

The suspense is killing me.

DIALOG

A : 내가 당신에게 말을 해 줘도 믿지 않을걸.

You wouldn't believe me if I told you.

B : 하여튼 말해 줘요. **애타 죽겠어요.**

Tell me anyway. **The suspense is killing me.**

309 약을 지어 주세요
have prescription filled

DIALOG 1

A : **약을 좀 지어 주시겠어요.**
I'd like to **have this prescription filled**.

B : 알았어요. 곧 가지고 올게요.
OK. I'll have it for you right away.

DIALOG 2

A : 어떻게 오셨나요?
May I help you?

B : 이 처방으로 **약을 지어 주세요.**
Please **fill this prescription**.

310 약
medication

DIALOG

A : 독감 **약이** 좀 필요한데요.
Excuse me, I'd like some **medication** for a bad cold.

B : 네. 증세가 어때요?
All right. What are your symptoms?

A : 온몸이 쑤시고 콧물이 나와요.
I ache all over and have a runny nose.

311 약물 중독자
drug addict

DIALOG

A : 그의 아버지에게 무슨 일이 있니?

What's the matter with his father?

B : 그의 아버지는 **약물 중독자야**.

He's **a drug addict**.

312 어디까지 했지요?

Where was I?

DIALOG

A : **어디까지 이야기했지요**?

Where was I?

B : 정원 가꾸기에 대한 이야기를 하셨어요.

You were talking about gardening.

313 어색하다

feel like a fish out of water, feel ill at ease

DIALOG

A : 어제 저녁 파티에서 재미있었나요?

Did you have a good time at the party last night?

B : 부자들 틈에 끼어 물 떠난 물고기처럼 **어색했어요**.

No, **I felt like a fish out of water** among rich people.

[Note] a fish out of water 익숙한 자기 환경인 물속에 있지 못하고 바깥에 나온 물고기의 처지, 생각만 해도 재미있는 표현이다.

314 어수선하다

a mess

DIALOG

A : 책상이 꽤 **어수선하네**. 정리 좀 했으면 좋겠어.

Your desk is a mess, I want you to get organized.

B : 미안해요. 곧 치울게요.

I'm sorry. I'll clean it right away.

315 어울리다

look good on someone

DIALOG

A : 내 콧수염 어때?

How do you like my mustache?

B : 솔직히 말해서 **전혀 어울리지 않아**.

Frankly, **it doesn't look good on you at all**.

316 어지르다

mess up

DIALOG

A : 네가 신경을 건드리는구나.

You're getting on my nerves.

B : 어떻게요?

How?

A : 이 방을 온통 **어질러 놨잖아**.

You've **messed up** this whole room.

317 어째서(왜)

How come?

DIALOG 1

A : **왜** 늦었니?

How come you're late?

B : 교통이 혼잡해서요.

The traffic was bad.

DIALOG 2

A : 그녀에게 식사하러 가자고 청한 걸로 알고 있는데, 어떻게 되었니?

I know you asked her out to dinner. How did it go?

B : 거절당했어요.

She turned me down.

A : 안됐군, **어째서지**?

That's too bad, **how come**?

[Note] turn down = reject 거절하다/Henry tried to join the army but was turned down because of a weak heart. 헨리는 군에 입대하려고 했으나 심장이 약하다는 이유로 거절당했다.

318 얼빠진 표정을 짓다

have a blank look

DIALOG

A : 왜 그렇게 **얼빠진(멍청한) 표정을 짓고 있니**?

Why do you **have such a blank look on your face**?

B : 한 시간 전에 약속이 있었던 것이 이제야 생각났어.

I just remembered that I had an appointment an hour ago.

[Note] blank 얼빠진, 멍청한, 생기가 없는

319 얼음 넣은 위스키

a whisky on the rocks

DIALOG

A : **얼음 넣은 위스키** 한 잔 주세요.

Give me a **whisky on the rocks**, please.

B : 곧 가져올게요.

Coming right up.

[Note] on the rocks (위스키 따위에) 얼음만 넣은(물이나 다른 음료를 타지 않은)

320 얼핏 생각으로는

off the top of my head, off-hand

DIALOG

A : 회의에 몇 명이나 참석했나요?

How many people do you think attended the meeting?

B : **얼핏 생각으로는** 200여 명 출석한 것 같아요.

Offhand, I would say that there were about two hundred people present.

321 여기저기(여러 군데) 알아보다

shop around

DIALOG

A : 업자를 고용하기 전에 **여러 군데 알아보셨나요**?

Did you **shop around** before hiring a contractor?

B : 네, 그럼요. 사실 견적서를 3개나 받아 중간 가격으로 결정했어요.

Yes, I did. As a matter of fact, I got three estimates and went for the middle price.

A : 왜 최저 가격을 안하고요?

Why not the lowest one?

B : 싸구려 가격에 싸구려 작업이 걱정돼서요.

Because I was afraid of a cheap job at a cheap price.

[Note] go for~ ~에 찬성하다, 의지하다

322 역전승하다
come from behind and win

DIALOG

A : 어제 저녁 A와 B의 경기 TV에서 보았어요?

Did you watch the A and B game on TV last night?

B : 아니요. 누가 이겼어요?

No, I didn't. Who won?

A : A가 6대 5로 **역전승했어요**.

A **came from behind and won** 6:5.

[Note] "역전승하다"를 win a come-from-behind victory라 해도 된다.

323 연속극
soap(opera)

DIALOG

A : **연속극** 중에 재미있는 것도 몇 있어요.

Some of the **soaps** are really interesting.

B : 농담하시는 거지요.

You must be kidding.

A : 아니요. 나는 '제너럴 호스피털'의 팬이에요.

No, I'm not. I'm a fan of General Hospital.

324 연습은 완벽을 낳는다

Practice makes perfect.

DIALOG

A : 이것은 나에게 확실히 불가능해요.

This is certainly impossible for me.

B : 기억하세요, **연습은 완벽을 낳는다는 걸.**

Remember, **practice makes perfect.**

325 예행 연습을 하다

rehearse

DIALOG

A : 연극 준비는 다 되었나요?

Is the play ready to open?

B : 네, 하지만 **예행 연습을 할** 시간이 더 있으면 좋겠어요.

Yes, but I wish we had more time to **rehearse.**

[Note] rehearse a wedding ceremony 결혼식 예행 연습을 하다.

326 열이 있다

run a temperature(fever)

DIALOG

A : **몸에 열이 있는 데다** 목도 심하게 아파요.

I've **been running a fever (temperature)** and I have a sore throat.

B : 처방해 줄 테니 동네 약국에서 약을 짓도록 하세요.

I'll give you a prescription that you can have filled at your local drug-store.

327 열성(열심)을 쏟다

put in all the hard work

DIALOG 1

A : 결국 승진이 됐다는 것을 믿을 수가 없어요.

I can't believe my promotion finally came through.

B : 당신이 쏟은 모든 **열성을 봐서** 그건 당연해요.

You deserve it after **all the hard work you've put in**.

DIALOG 2

A : "뜻이 있는 곳에 길이 있다"는 격언은 무슨 뜻이지?

What does the saying "Where there is a will, there is a way" mean?

B : 우리가 **열성을 쏟으면** 이루지 못할 일이 없다는 뜻이야.

It means there is nothing we can't accomplish when we **put in all the hard work**.

A : 아, 그렇구나.

I see.

328 엿듣다(도청하다)

listen in on one's conversation, eavesdrop on one's conversation

DIALOG

A : 어떻게 감히 우리 이야기를 **엿듣지요**?

How dare you **eavesdrop on** our conversation?

B : 아니 **엿듣지 않았어요**, 정말이에요. 당신이 이야기하고 있는 것을 알고 곧 (수화기를) 놓았어요.

I **didn't listen in on your conversation**, honest! I got off as soon as I found out you were on.

[Note] listen in on~ = eavesdrop on~ = overhear~ 엿듣다, 도청하다

329 예감이 들다
have a hunch

DIALOG

A : 오늘 나에게 뭔가 나쁜 일이 생길 것 같은 **예감이 드는데.**

I **have a hunch** that something bad is going to happen to me today.

B : 왜요?

Why?

A : 어젯밤 꿈이 나빴어요.

I had a bad dream last night.

B : 바보 같은 생각 말아요. 꿈은 아무 의미가 없어요.

Oh, don't be silly. Dreams don't mean anything.

[Note] 네가 올 것 같은 예감이 들었다. I had a hunch that you would come.

330 예산대로 살다
be on a budget

DIALOG

A : **예산대로 살면** 돈을 저축할 수 있어요.

You can save money if **you're on a budget**.

B : 맞아요. 우리는 **예산을 세우고** 사치품을 사지 않아요.

You're right. **We're on a budget** and we don't buy luxuries.

[Note] 우리 예산에 맞다. It suits our budget. 예산 중 가장 큰 항목은 무엇입니까? What is the biggest item in your budget?

331 어느 정도 예산하고 있나요?
What price range do you have in mind?

DIALOG

A : 우리는 식탁을 하나 찾고 있어요.
We're looking for a dining table.

B : **어느 정도 예산하셨나요**?
What price range did you have in mind?

332 예약이 다 되다
We're all booked up.

DIALOG 1

A : 오늘 저녁에 더블 침대 빈 것 있어요?
Do you have any doubles available for tonight?

B : 미안합니다만 **예약이 다 되었어요**.
I'm sorry, **we're all booked up**.

DIALOG 2

A : 오늘 저녁 7시에 6명 앉을 테이블 하나 예약하고 싶어요.
I'd like to reserve a table for six for 7 o'clock tonight.

B : 미안합니다. 7시에는 모두 **예약이 되었네요**. 5시나 8시 예약은 가능합니다.
Sorry, sir, all tables are **booked up** for 7 o'clock. Reservations are available for five or eight.

A : 좋아요. 그럼 8시로 하지요.
Good. Make it 8:00 then.

333 예약하다
reserve(book), make a reservation

DIALOG

A : 내일 아침 제주행 비행기 **예약하고 싶어요**.

I'd like to book a seat on tomorrow morning's flight to Jeju.

B : 누구 이름으로 할까요?

What name is it under?

334 예외를 만들다

make an exception

DIALOG

A : 제발 좀 봐 주세요.

Please have a heart, will you?

B : 당신이라고 **예외를 만들 수는** 없어요. 미안합니다. 절차가 그래서요.

I can't **make an exception**. I'm sorry. That's just the way it is.

[Note] 모든 법칙에는 예외가 있다. Every rule has its exceptions.
이 규칙에는 하나의 예외가 있다. There is one exception to this rule.

335 예정대로

on schedule

DIALOG

A : **예정대로** 비행하고 있습니까?

Are we flying **on schedule**?

B : 네, 뉴욕에 오전 8시 30분에 도착 예정입니다.

Yes. It's scheduled to arrive in New York at 8:30 a.m.

336 예측하기 어렵다

It's a toss-up.

DIALOG

A : 라이온스 팀과 타이거 팀 중 누가 이길 거라고 생각하나요?

Who do you think is going to win, the Lions or the Tigers?

B : **예측하기 어려운데요.**

I think it's a toss-up.

[Note] 그가 올지 안 올지는 단정할 수 없다.

It's a toss-up whether he will come or not.

337 옛날 것의

outdated

DIALOG

A : 이 신청서 사용할 수 있나요?

Can I use these applications?

B : 아니요, 그것들은 **옛날 거예요**. 여기 새 신청서가 있어요.

No. They're **outdated**. We have new ones here.

338 오늘은 이만 끝냅시다

Let's call it a day.

DIALOG

A : 지금 몇 시지?

What time is it?

B : 5시 10분이에요.

It's ten after five, sir.

A : 벌써? 그러면 **오늘은 이만합시다.**

Already? **Let's call it a day**, then.

339 오래 걸리다

be long

DIALOG

A : 사장님은 지금 다른 분과 이야기 중인데, 좀 기다려 주시겠어요?

Our boss is with someone else right now. Can you wait?

B : 네, **오래 걸릴까요**?

Yes. Do you think **he'll be long**?

A : 아니요, 몇 분만 있으면 끝날 거예요.

No. He should be free in just a few minutes.

340 왜 오래 걸리셨어요?

What took you so long?

DIALOG

A : **왜 그렇게 오래 걸리셨어요**?

What took you so long?

B : 고속도로에서 교통 체증에 걸렸어요.

I got held up in traffic on the free way.

341 오랜만이야

Long time no see

DIALOG

A : 너를 우연히 만나다니, 뜻밖이구나!

What a pleasant surprise running into you!

B : **오랜만이군**. 어떻게 지냈니?

Long time no see. How've you been?

342 오해하다

get a person wrong

DIALOG

A : 제가 구두쇠란 말인가요?

Are you saying I'm a cheapskate?

B : **오해하지 마세요**. 제 말은 매우 검소하다는 뜻이에요.

Don't get me wrong. I just meant to say that you are very frugal.

343 (~로) 옷을 갈아입다

change into~

DIALOG 1

A : 오늘 이 옷을 입어도 괜찮을까요?

Do you think I can wear this today?

B : 좀 더 점잖은 것으로 **갈아입는 게** 좋겠어요

You'd better **change into** a little more formal dress.

DIALOG 2

A : 오늘도 또 덥겠군.

I think we're in for another hot day today.

B : 그럼 우리 짧은 바지로 **갈아입을까**?

Shall we **change into** shorts?

344 왕복인가요, 편도인가요

One way or round trip?

DIALOG

A : 제주도 예약을 하려고 합니다.

I'd like to make a reservation to Jeju Island.

B : **편도인가요, 왕복인가요?**

One way or round trip?

A : **왕복으로 해 주세요.**

Make it a round trip, please.

345 외모가 형편없다

not much to look at

DIALOG

A : 그의 여자 친구는 정말 못생겼어요

His girl friend is really ugly.

B : 알아요, 그의 **외모도 정말 형편없어요.**

I know, and **he's not much to look at**, either.

346 외상이에요, 현금이에요

charge or cash?

DIALOG

A : **외상입니까, 현금입니까?**

Is this charge or cash?

B : 제 비자 카드로 올려 주세요.

You can put it on my VISA card.

347 요기하다

have a bite to eat, little something

DIALOG

A : 별로 배가 고프지는 않지만 **요기만 했으면** 좋겠어.

I'm not very hungry, but I would like **a little something**.

B : 좋아, 영화가 끝나면 잠깐 들러서 **요기나 하자.**

Okay. After the movie, we'll stop and **have a bite to eat.**

348 요령을 터득하다

get the knack (hang) of~

DIALOG 1

A : 연습을 계속하면 **요령을 터득하게 돼.**

Keep practicing, you'll **get the knack of** it.

B : 알았어요, **요령을 알 것 같아요.**

I see. I think I'm **getting the hang of** it.

DIALOG 2

A : 그것을 어떻게 작동하나요? 굉장히 복잡한 것 같은데요.

How do you operate it? It looks so complicated.

B : 하지만 일단 **요령을 터득하면** 그렇게 어렵지 않아요.

It is, but once you **get the hang of** it, it's not as difficult as it looks.

349 요점을 말하다

come (get) to the point

DIALOG

A : 제가 지적해야 할 점이 몇 가지 있어요.

There are a few things I should point out.

B : 좋아요, 하지만 돌려서 말하지 말고 **요점만 말씀하세요.** 시간이 많지 않으니까요.

OK, but don't beat around the bush. **Get to the point.** We don't have all day.

350 요행을 바라다
take a chance

DIALOG

A : 혹시 지금 7명 앉을 테이블이 있나요?
Do you by any chance have a table for seven available?

B : 2, 3분 후에 날 것 같으니 좀 기다려 주시겠어요?
A table will be available in a few minutes. Would you like to wait?

A : 물론이죠. **요행을 바라고** 들어오길 잘했군요.
Sure. I'm glad I **took a chance**.

351 용건
the nature of your business

DIALOG

A : 갤러웨이 박사를 좀 만날 수 있을까요? 약속은 하지 않았는데요.
May I see Dr. Galloway? I don't have an appointment.

B : 무슨 **용건인지** 말씀해 주시겠어요?
May I ask you **the nature of your business**, sir?

A : 글쎄요, 사적인 건데요. 그는 저를 알 거예요.
Well. It's kind of personal. He knows me.

[Note] kind of~ 약간, 좀

352 용기를 내다
summon up one's courage, find nerve(courage)

DIALOG

A : 당신의 큰 문제는 무엇인가요?

What's your big problem?

B : 그녀에게 구혼할 **용기가 나지 않아요.**

I **can't find the nerve (courage)** to propose to her.

(혹은 I can never **bring myself to** ask for her hand.)

[Note] 구혼하다 ask for one's hand, propose to~/Somehow he could never summon up the courage to ask for her hand. 어찌된 영문인지 그는 그녀에게 구혼할 용기를 낼 수 없었다.

353 우등으로 졸업하다

graduate with honors

DIALOG

A : 그는 고등학교를 **우등으로 졸업했어요.**

He **graduated** from high school **with honors.**

B : 열심히 공부한 성과가 있었군요.

His hard work has paid off.

354 우선

to start with

DIALOG

A : 제가 무엇을 할까요?

What do you want me to do?

B : **우선** 진공 청소기로 청소 좀 해 줘요.

I want you to vacuum the house **to start with.**

355 우선적인 것

the first priority

DIALOG

A : 아이들에게 성실함을 가르치는 것이 매우 중요해요.

Teaching children a sense of integrity is very important.

B : 저도 그것이 제일 **우선적이라고** 생각해요.

I think it's **the first priority**.

[Note] 오늘 저녁 만사를 제쳐놓고라도 공부를 해야 해. Tonight, studying is my first (top) priority. / 소방차가 모든 차량보다 우선이다. Fire engines have priority over other traffic.

356 우연의 일치

coincidence

DIALOG

A : 그의 이름이 당신 이름과 똑같군요.

His name is identical to yours.

B : 농담이 아니고요? **무슨 우연의 일치람!**

No kidding? **What a coincidence!**

357 우연히 만나다

run into~

DIALOG

A : **우연히 만나다니**, 뜻밖이군요.

What a pleasant surprise **running into you!**

B : 오랜만이에요. 어떻게 지냈어요?

Long time no see. How've you been!

358 우울하다

have the blues, sad, gloomy in spirits

DIALOG 1

A : 기분이 저조해 보이네요.

You look depressed.

B : 그래요, 오늘 기분이 정말 **우울해요**.

I am, I really **have the blues** today.

DIALOG 2

A : 왜 **우울한 얼굴**을 하고 있어요?

Why **the long face**? (Why do you look so blue? = Why are you in a blue mood?)

B : 오늘 큰 실수를 했어요.

I made a big mistake today.

A : 엎질러진 물을 어쩌겠어요. 밝은 면을 보도록 해요. 구름에도 밝은 면은 있는 법이니까요.

No use crying over spilled milk. Try to look on the bright side. Every cloud has a silver lining.

359 운에 맡기고 해 보다

run the risk, try (take) the chance

DIALOG

A : 하룻밤 묵을 방이 있을까요?

Do you have a room available for one night?

B : 지금 당장은 없지만, 한 시간 기다릴 수 있어요?

Not right now. Could you wait for one hour?

A : 물론이죠. **운에 맡기고 해 보길 잘했군**.

Sure. **I'm glad I took the chance**.

360 운이 없는 걸요

Just my luck!

DIALOG 1

A : 미안합니다. 좋은 기회를 놓쳤군요. 세일은 어제 끝났어요.

Sorry, you missed the boat. The sale ended yesterday.

B : 그래요? 내가 **운이 없어 그런 걸요.**

Really? **Just my luck!**

[Note] miss the boat 좋은 기회를 놓치다.

DIALOG 2

A : 겨우 숫자 하나가 틀려 백만 불짜리 복권을 놓치다니, 참 안됐군요.

Too bad you missed the million dollar lottery by just one digit.

B : 글쎄요, 내가 **운이 없어 그런 걸요.**

Well, **that's just my luck.**

[Note] It was just my luck to marry him in the first place. 애당초부터 그하고 결혼한 것이 다 내 팔자지요./digit 아라비아 숫자 0에서 9까지.

361 운동하다

work out

DIALOG 1

A : 건강해 보이는군요, 건강을 위해 **운동하나요**?

You are in good shape. Do you **work out** to keep in shape?

B : 네, 헬스클럽에서 격일로 **운동해요.**

Yes, I **work out** every other day at a health club.

DIALOG 2

A : **운동을 하고 있지요**. 그렇죠?

You work out, don't you?

B : 어떻게 알아요?

How do you know that?

A : 체격을 보고서요. 체격이 좋군요.

From your physique. You have a nice build.

362 웃음거리가 되다

make a fool of oneself

DIALOG

A : 왜 학교 연극에 참석하지 않아요?

Why do you refuse to take part in the school play?

B : **웃음거리가 될 게** 뻔하니까요.

Because I'm sure that **I'll simply make a fool of myself**.

363 원예 솜씨가 좋다

have a green thumb

DIALOG 1

A : 이 정원은 **원예 솜씨가 좋다든가** 운이 좋은 결과는 아니에요.

This garden is not the result of **a green thumb** or luck.

B : 그래요?

It isn't?

A : 제 말을 믿으세요. 정원을 가꾸는 데는 손이 많이 가거든요.

Take my word for it, gardening requires a lot of work.

DIALOG 2

A : 부인은 **원예 솜씨가 좋은 것 같군요**. 집안 식물들이 아름답게 자라는 걸 보면요.

Your wife seems to **have a green thumb**, all her house plants grow beautifully.

B : 그렇기도 하지만 원예는 손도 많이 간답니다.

She sure does, but gardening requires a lot of work, too.

364 원하는 대로 하다
Suit yourself.

DIALOG
A : 영화를 보러 가는 대신 쇼핑 가는 것이 어때요?

I would like to go shopping instead of going to the movies.

B : **원하는 대로 해요.**

Suit yourself.

365 월급
monthly pay

DIALOG 1
A : **월급이** 얼마나 됩니까?

How much is your **monthly pay**?

B : 쥐꼬리만 해요. 5명의 우리 가족에는 간에 기별도 안 가지요.

Chicken feed. It's practically a drop in the bucket for my family of five.

[Note] chicken feed 소량의 돈(닭모이 정도)/a drop in the bucket 굉장히 작은 양(양동이 속의 물 한 방울)

DIALOG 2
A : **실제 손에 들어오는 월급은** 얼마예요?

How much is **your take-home pay**?

B : 글쎄요, 저는 1주에 100불을 버는데 집에 가지고 가는 것은 87불 정도예요.

Well, I earn $100 dollars a week, but my take-home pay is

only $87.

[Note] take-home pay (세금 따위를 제한) 실제 손에 들어오는 급료

366 위로하다(위안이 되다)
cheer one up

DIALOG

A : 이 꽃들 예쁘네요. 당신의 깊은 배려에 진심으로 감사드립니다.
These flowers are beautiful. I really appreciate your thoughtfulness.

B : 감사합니다. 당신이 편찮으신 동안 이 꽃들이 **위안이 되리라** 생각해요.
Thank you. I thought they might **cheer you up** while you're sick.

367 유머 감각이 있다
have sense of humor

DIALOG

A : 누구나 그를 아주 좋아하는 것을 보았어요.
I've noticed that everyone likes him very much.

B : 그의 **유머 감각 때문에** 주위 사람들이 그와 같이 있고 싶어해요.
His **sense of humor** makes him really fun to be around.

368 유행하다
go around

DIALOG

A : 감기에 걸린 것 같군요.
It sounds like you're coming down with a cold.

B : 그런 것 같아요.

I'm afraid so.

A : 조심해야 해요. **감기가 유행하고 있어요.**

You'd better take care. **There's a lot of colds going around.**

[Note] come down with~ ~에 걸리다(병).

369 유행에 뒤떨어진
out of style

DIALOG 1

A : 당신 그런 모자를 쓰려고 하는 것은 아니지요?

You're not going to wear those hats, are you?

B : 그것이 어때서요?

What's wrong with them?

A : **유행에 뒤떨어졌어요.**

They're out of style.

DIALOG 2

B : 저 상점에서 물건을 사고 싶지 않아요.

I don't like to shop in that store.

A : 나도 싫어요, 그 상점에서는 **최신 유행을 따라가지 못해요.**

I don't, either. He **doesn't keep up with the latest styles.**

370 언제까지 유효한가요?
When is it good through?

DIALOG

A : 어떻게 지불하시겠어요?

How are you going to pay?

B : 비자를 쓸게요.

Charge it to my VISA card.

A : **언제까지 유효한가요?**

When is it good through? (혹은 **When is the expiration date?**)

371 응석을 받아주다

pamper

DIALOG

A : 아기 **응석을** 지나치게 **받아 주지 마세요.**

Don't pamper your baby too much.

B : 그렇게 **응석을 받아 주는** 것도 없어요.

I'm not **pampering** him that much.

[Note] pamper 지나치게 아끼다, 제멋대로 하게 하다, 응석받다.

372 의견 대립이 많다

We have a lot of disagreement.

DIALOG

A : 왜 남자 친구한테 화가 났나요?

Why are you angry with your boy-friend?

B : 말로 표현하기 어렵지만 **의견 대립이 많아요.**

It's hard to put into words, but **we've had a lot of disagreement.**

[Note] put into words 말로 표현하다

373 의견을 말할 권리가 있다

be entitled to one's opinion(voice one's opinion)

DIALOG 1

A : 당신 기분을 상하게 하지 않았기를 바래요.

I hope I didn't offend you.

B : 괜찮아요. **당신도 자신의 의견을 말할 수 있는 권리가 있지요.**

That's all right. **You're entitled to your opinion.**

DIALOG 2

A : 왜 그렇게 말이 많지요?

Why do you talk so much?

B : **제 의견을 말할 권리가 있어요.**

I'm entitled to voice my opinion.

[Note] be entitled to~ ~을 받을 자격(권리)이 있다/be entitled to praise 칭찬을 받을 자격이 있다/voice one's opinion 의견을 말하다

374 (그럴) 의도는 전혀 없다

have no intention of~

DIALOG

A : 그를 기분 나쁘게 하지 마세요.

Don't cause him to get upset.

B : 그럴 **의도는 전혀 없어요.**

I **don't have any intention** of doing that.

375 (~할) 의무가 있다

have an obligation

DIALOG

A : 당신은 그에게 무슨 **의무라도 있나요?**

Do you **have any obligation** to him?

B : 아니요, **의무 같은 것은 없지만** 그냥 돕고 싶어요.

No, **I have no obligation**, but I just want to help him.

376 의식이 들다

come to (one's senses), regain consciousness

DIALOG

A : 그가 기절했어요.

He passed out.

B : 찬물을 좀 부어요. 그러면 **의식이 들 거예요**.

Pour some cold water on him, and he will **come to**.

[Note] pass out 의식을 잃다, 기절하다. 술을 마시고 정신을 잃다.

377 이륙하다

take off

DIALOG 1

A : 비행기가 몇 시에 **이륙하나요**?

What time is the plane going to **leave**?

B : 10시 30분에 **이륙해요.**

It'll **take off** at 10:30.

DIALOG 2

A : 저건 무슨 방송이지요?

What's that announcement?

B : **이륙이** 2시간 늦어진다는 거예요

Take off will be delayed for two hours.

[Note] take off가 동사일 경우와 명사인 경우가 있다. / 이륙시에는 금연입니다. No

smoking during take off.

378 이야기를 꾸며내다
make up a story

DIALOG

A : 그를 만나면 이야깃거리가 없어서 걱정이에요.

I'm afraid I have nothing to talk about with him when I meet him.

B : 그러면 **이야기를 꾸며내지 그래**, 즉흥적으로 아무거나.

Then, why don't you **make something up**–anything off the top of your head.

[Note] off the top of one's head 즉흥적으로, 당장 머리에 떠오르는

379 이유를 대다
give a good reason

DIALOG

A : 왜 늦었는지 **납득할 만한 이유를 대 봐.**

Give me a good reason why you're late.

B : 교통이 막혔어요.

I was caught in traffic.

[Note] in the traffic이라 하지 않고 in traffic이라 쓴다.

380 이익을 보다
make a good profit, come out with a good profit

DIALOG 1

A : 이것으로 틀림없이 돈을 벌 수 있을까요?

Are you sure we can make any money on this?

B : 틀림없이 많은 **이익을 볼 수 있을 겁니다.**

I'm sure we'll **make a good profit on** this one.

DIALOG 2

A : 총경비가 너무 비싸서 **이익을 거의 보지 못했어요.**

Overhead has been so high that **we show very little profit.**

B : 임시로 직원을 해고할 생각은 해 보았나요?

Have you considered laying off some workers?

[Note] overhead 총경비, 총비용/lay off 임시로 해고하다(불경기로)

381 일이 밀려 있다

be behind in one's work, be up to one's ears in work

DIALOG 1

A : 제주도로 피서 갑시다.

Let's go to Jeju Island for the summer.

B : 갈 수 있다면 얼마나 좋겠어요. 하지만 할 **일이 밀려 있어요.**

I wish I could, but **I'm behind in my work.** (혹은 **I'm up to my ears in work.**)

DIALOG 2

A : 쇼핑 갑시다.

Let's go shopping.

B : **설거지할 것이 많아서 갈 수 없어요.**

I can't, I'm up to my elbows in dirty dishes.

382 일을 열심히 하다

work one's fingers to the bone(= work one's head off)

DIALOG

A : 나는 요즘 저녁 때만 되면 몹시 피곤해요.

I've been tired out in the evening lately.

B : 일을 **열심히 하니까** 그렇지요.

It's because you've been **working your head off**.(혹은 **working your fingers to the bone**.)

[Note] work one's head (tail) off 열심히 일하다/work one's fingers to the bone 몸을 아끼지 않고 일하다

383 일행이 몇 분인가요?

How large is your party?

DIALOG

A : 오늘 저녁 식사 테이블을 하나 예약하고 싶어요.

I'd like to reserve a table for dinner tonight.

B : **일행이 몇 분인가요**?

How large is your party, sir?(= **How many are in your group**?)

A : 일곱 명이에요.

Seven.(We are a party of seven.)

B : 누구 이름으로 해 둘까요?

What name is it under?

384 임신 중이다

be expecting(pregnant)

DIALOG

A : 언니는 어떻게 지내니?

How is your sister?

B : 지금 **임신 중이야.**

She is **expecting(pregnant).** 혹은 She **is going to have a baby.**

A : 그럼 입덧도 하고 아이스크림이나 피클을 먹고 싶어 하겠군요.

Then she must have morning sickness and cravings.

[Note] morning sickness (임신한 여자에게 생기는) 아침 구토증, 입덧/They have morning sickness = They are sick in the mornings/craving (강한) 욕구, 열망, 동경, 간청, Pregnant women crave ice-cream and pickles. 임신한 여성 들은 아이스크림이나 피클 등을 먹고 싶어 한다.

385 입만 가지고 오세요(그냥 오기만 하세요)

Just bring yourself.

DIALOG

A : 저도 무엇을 좀 가져오게 해 주세요.

Let me bring something.

B : **입만 가지고 오세요(그냥 오시기만 하세요).**

Just bring yourself.

386 입이 가벼운 사람

a blabber-mouth

DIALOG

A : 그것이 공식적으로 발표되기까지는 아무에게도 말하지 마세요. 소문이 나면 일을 망쳐 버릴지도 모르니까요.

Don't tell anyone until it's official. Rumors may ruin the whole thing.

B : 알겠어요, 저는 **입이 가벼운 사람이** 아닙니다.

No, I won't. I'm not **a blabber-mouth**.

387 (깜빡) 잊다

slip one's mind

DIALOG

A : 교수님의 성함이 무엇입니까?

What's your professor's name?

B : 혀 끝에 뱅뱅 도는데 **깜빡 잊었어요**. 잠깐만요, 생각날 거예요.

It's on the tip of my tongue, but it **slipped my mind.**

Just a minute. It'll come to me.

자

388 자격이 있다

have qualification, deserve

DIALOG 1

A : 오늘 취업 면접이 걱정되네요.

I'm worried about the job interview today.

B : 그것에 대해서는 걱정할 필요 없어요. **굉장한 자격을 갖고 있으니까요.**

You don't have to worry: you **have very impressive qualification.**

DIALOG 2

A : 나이 많으신 분들은 우리 동네에서 특별 대접을 받아요.

Old people are treated with special attention in our community.

B : 그들은 그럴 만한 **자격이 있지요.**

They **deserve** it.

389 자명종이 울리지 않았다

My alarm clock didn't go off.

DIALOG

A : 어떻게 늦잠을 자게 되었어요?

How come you overslept?

B : **자명종이 울리지 않았어요.**

My alarm clock didn't go off.

390 자리를 비우다
be gone

DIALOG 1

A : 30분 이상이나 **자리를 비웠는데** 왜 그렇게 오래 걸렸어요?

You **were gone** for more than 30 minutes.

What took you so long?

B : 심한 독감으로 병원에 다녀왔어요.

I have a terrible cold so I went to see my doctor.

DIALOG 2

A : 지금까지 어디에 있었어요?

Where have you been all this time?

B : 이봐요, 30분밖에 **자리를 비우지** 않았어요.

Look, I **was** only **gone** for half an hour.

[Note] 자리를 얼마나 비울 거예요? How long will you be gone?

391 자리에 없습니다
be not available

DIALOG

A : 사장님 좀 바꿔 주세요.

May I speak to your boss?

B : **자리에 안 계시는데요.** 전하실 말씀 있으세요?

He's not available. Would you like to leave a message?

392 자업자득이다
That's what you get for~

DIALOG

A : 내 친구들은 나와 자리를 함께하는 걸 좋아하지 않아요.

My friends don't welcome my company anymore.

B : 그건 당신이 이기적인 것에서 오는 **자업자득이에요.**

That's what you get for being so selfish.

393 작업 교체가 시작되다

workshift starts(begins)

DIALOG

A : 저 인부들은 왜 서성대고 있나요?

Why are those workers just standing around?

B : **작업 교체가 시작될** 때까지 시간을 메꾸고 있는 거예요.

They're killing time until their **workshift starts.**

394 잔소리가 미치게 하다

one's nagging drives one crazy

DIALOG

A : 그녀의 무엇이 당신을 괴롭히나요?

What is it about her that bothers you?

B : 그 여자의 끊임없는 **잔소리가 나를 미치게 한답니다.**

Her constant **nagging drives me crazy.**

395 잠을 푹 자다

have a good night's sleep

DIALOG

A : 간밤에 **푹 주무셨어요?**

Good morning. Did you **have a good night's sleep?**

B : 아니요, 한잠도 못 잤어요. 오늘 취업 면접 생각하느라고 엎치락뒤치락했지요.

No, I didn't sleep a wink. I tossed and turned all night thinking about today's job interview.

[Note] don't sleep a wink 한숨도 못 자다/toss and turn all night 밤새도록 엎치락뒤치락하다.

396 (깜빡) 잠이 들다

doze off

DIALOG

A : 왜 그렇게 늦었어요?

Why are you so late?

B : 버스에서 **깜빡 잠이 들어** 정류장을 지나 버렸어요.

I **dozed off** on the bus and missed my stop.

397 장난하다

play a trick on, fool around

DIALOG 1

A : 네가 모두 A를 받았다고 담임 선생님이 말씀하셨어.

Your teacher told me you got all A's.

B : **장난으로 그러시는 거지요**?

Are you **playing a trick on** me?

A : 아니, 진담이야.

No, I'm serious.

DIALOG 2

A : TV 가지고 **장난하지 마**.

Don't fool around with the TV.

B : 영상을 맞추려고 그래요.

I'm trying to adjust the picture.

DIALOG 3

A : 그 칼 가지고 **장난하지 마.**

Don't fool around with that knife.

B : 조심하고 있으니 괜찮아요.

It's OK, I'm being careful.

398 재미있는

lots of fun

DIALOG

A : 그는 어떤 사람이에요?

What kind of a person is he?

B : 훌륭한 분이지요, **재미 있고.** 당신도 그를 좋아하게 될 거예요.

He's a great person, and **lots of fun.** You're bound to like him.

399 재촉하다(다그치다)

be pushy

DIALOG 1

A : 빨리빨리요, 늦겠어요.

Hurry up, hurry up. We'll be late!

B : **재촉하지 말아요.**

Don't be so pushy!

DIALOG 2

A : 숙제를 좀 도와줘요!

Please help me with my homework!

B : 알았어요. 도와줄게요. 그런데 너무 **재촉하는군요**.

OK. I'll help you get your paper done, but **you're being awfully pushy**.

400 저의가 무엇인가요?

What's your ulterior motive?

DIALOG

A : **당신의 저의가 무엇인가요?**

What's your ulterior motive?

B : 당신을 도와주고 싶을 뿐이에요.

I just want to help you with it, that's all.

401 전구를 끼다

put in a light bulb

DIALOG

A : 저 희미한 불 좀 어떻게 해 봐요.

I wish you would do something about that dim light.

B : 더 밝은 **전구를** 끼울게요.

I'll put in a stronger **light bulb**.

[Note] strong (빛 색깔 따위가) 강렬한, a strong light 강한 빛

402 전근되다

be transferred

DIALOG

A : 만일 네가 부산지점으로 **전근되면** 누가 지배인 자리를 맡을 건가?

If you **are transferred to** the Busan branch, who's going to take over your position as the manager?

B : 아직 미정이야.

It's still up in the air.

403 (한국 음식을) 전문으로 하다

Their specialty is Korean dishes.

DIALOG

A : 서양 요리도 있습니까?

Do they have any Western dishes?

B : 네, 있습니다만 한국 음식을 **전문**으로 합니다.

Yes, they do, but their **specialty** is Korean.

404 전부 다

The works

DIALOG 1

A : 햄버거를 어떻게 해 드릴까요?

What would you like on your hamburger?

B : **전부 다** 넣어 주세요.

I want everything on it, **the works**. (혹은 간단히) **The works**.

DIALOG 2

A : 30달러를 내면 무엇무엇을 해 주나요?

What does the 30 dollars include?

B : 오일교환, 그리스, 에어필터를 **전부** 드려요.

An oil change, grease, new air filter, **the works**.

[Note] I wanted to look particularly well that evening, so I told the barber to give me the works; shave, haircut, shampoo, tonic, etc. 그날 저녁은 특별히 미남으로 보이고 싶어서 이발사에게 면도, 머리깎기, 샴푸, 토닉 등 몽땅 해 달라고 했다.

405 전화를 끊다
hang up

DIALOG

A : 그녀는 내가 한 말에 화가 났음에 틀림없어.
She must be very angry at what I said.

B : 왜요?
Why?

A : 통화 중에 무례하게 **끊어 버렸어**.
She **hung up** on me.

406 (통화 도중) 전화가 끊기다
be disconnected, be cut off

DIALOG

A : 한국과 통화하던 **전화가 끊겼는데** 다시 연결해 주세요.
My call to Korea **has been cut off(= disconnected)**.
Please try to reconnect us.

B : 알았습니다. 몇 번과 통화하고 있었나요?
All right. What was the number you were calling?

407 전화를 연결해 주다
put your call through

DIALOG

A : 김 박사님 좀 부탁합니다.
May I speak to Dr. Kim?

B : **연결해 드리는** 동안 잠깐 기다려 주세요.

Hold on a minute (= moment) while I **put your call through.**

408 전화를 하고 있다(받고 있다)

be on the line

DIALOG

A : 김 교수님 좀 바꿔 주세요.

May I talk to Professor Kim?

B : 잠깐만 기다려 주세요. **다른 전화를 받고 있어요.**

Can you hold on a minute? **He's on the other line.**

409 (이상한) 전화가 많이 걸려오다

receive many crank (obscene) calls

DIALOG

A : 기분이 나빠요. 불쾌하고 이상한 **전화와** 잘못 걸려오는 전화가 많아요.

I'm upset. I've been receiving too many crank **phone calls** and wrong numbers.

B : 전화번호를 바꾸시지요.

Why don't you change your phone number?

410 놀라운 절경

absolutely breath-taking

DIALOG

A : 한국을 두루 여행할 기회가 있었나요?

Have you had the opportunity to travel around in Korea?

B : 네, 설악산에 갔었는데 정말 놀라운 **절경이었습니다.**

Yes. We've been to Mt. Sorak and found it absolutely **breathtaking.**

411 (오는 정이 있어야) 가는 정도 있다

Scratch my back and I'll scratch yours.

DIALOG

A : 제 부탁 하나 들어주세요.

Would you please do me a favor?

B : 네, 물론이죠. 뭔데요? **오는 정이 있으면 가는 정도 있다는** 격언을 알고 있어요.

Sure, what is it? I know the saying; **scratch my back and I'll scratch yours.**

412 정돈하다

get organized, straighten up

DIALOG 1

A : 제발 책상을 **정돈 안 된 상태로** 두지 말아라.

Please don't leave your desk **disorganized.**

(혹은 leave your desk **a mess.**)

B : 미안해요. 곧 **정돈할게요.**

I'm sorry. I'll **straighten it up** right now.

DIALOG 2

A : 이 물건들은 다 뭐지?

What's all this stuff?

B : 청소를 하고 있어요. 물건들을 버리고 **정리하고 있어요.**

I'm cleaning house. I'm going to get rid of things and **get organized.**

413 정말 그래요(맞는 말씀입니다)
You're telling me!

DIALOG

A : 여자 친구들과 데이트만 하지 말고 결혼하여 정착하지 그래요.
Why don't you marry and settle down instead of playing the field?

B : 적당한 여자를 만나지 못했어요. 그렇게 쉽지 않아요.
I haven't met Miss Right yet. It's not that easy to find a nice girl.

A : **정말 그래요.**
You're telling me!

414 정반대다
Quite the contrary

DIALOG

A : 그는 우리 학교 테니스 클럽 조직에 반대하고 있다던데.
I hear he is against the idea of organizing a tennis club in our school.

B : **정반대예요.** 그는 대찬성인데요.
Quite the contrary, he's all for it.

415 정상으로 돌아가다
be back to normal

DIALOG

A : 심한 독감을 앓았다면서? 지금은 어때?
I hear you've been suffering from a bad cold. How are you feeling now?

B : **정상으로 돌아왔지만** 무척 바빠요. 보충해야 할 학교 공부가 많아요.

Back to normal, but very busy. I have a lot of school work to make up.

416 정장으로 갈아입다

change into formal dress

DIALOG

A : 오늘 파티에 이렇게 입고 가도 될까요?

Do you think I should wear this to the party today?

B : **좀 더 정장으로 갈아입는 것이** 좋겠어요.

You'd better **change into something a little more formal.**

417 (~로) 정하다

settle for~

DIALOG

A : 초콜릿 아이스크림 있나요?

Could I have a chocolate ice-cream?

B : 미안합니다. 초콜릿이 다 떨어졌어요. 바닐라는 **어때요**?

Sorry. We're out of chocolate. Would you **settle for** vanilla?

[Note] settle for~ (원래는) ~로 만족하다(be content with)의 뜻. 3개 중에서 2개로만 정해 주세요. Would you settle for two out of three?

418 정확하지는 않지만(어림짐작이지만)

it's a long shot, but~

DIALOG

A : 결혼식에 몇 명이나 참석했어요?

How many people were there at the wedding?

B : **정확하지는 않지만** 약 1,000명쯤 됩니다.

I know **it's a long shot**, but I'll say 1,000.

C : 저도 그 정도 될 것으로 생각해요.

I'll go along with that.

[Note] go along with~ (의견 따위에) 찬성하여 따라가다

419 (내일 아침) 제일 먼저

the first thing tomorrow morning

DIALOG

A : 지금 당장 그 일을 했으면 좋겠어요.

I want you to get that thing done right away.

B : 내일 아침 일어나는 대로 **제일 먼저** 하면 안 될까요?

Can I do it **the first thing** tomorrow morning?

420 조급하게 굴지 마

Don't be so impatient.

DIALOG

A : **그렇게 조급하게 굴지 마.**

Don't be so impatient.(혹은 **There's no hurry.**)

B : 서둘러야 해요, 그렇지 않으면 늦어요.

Well, we have to hurry or we'll be late.

421 조립하다

assemble, put together

DIALOG

A : 이 장난감 차 **조립하는 것** 좀 도와주세요.

Can you help me **assemble** this toy car?

B : 물론이죠. 그런 거라면 잘 해요.

Sure. I'm good at that.

422 (마음이) 조마조마하다

be nervous, have butterflies in one's stomach

DIALOG

A : 초조한가요?

Are you nervous?

B : 네, **마음이 조마조마하군요**. 취업 면접 생각을 하니까.

Yes, I have **butterflies in my stomach** just thinking of having a job interview.

423 (어떤) 조처를 취하다

do something about~

DIALOG

A : 그들은 아들에 대하여 **어떤 조처를 취해야 할 거야**.

I think they have to **do something about** their son.

B : 당신 말이 맞아요. 만일 그 아이가 계속해서 그 아이들과 돌아다니면 결국 감방 신세를 지게 될 거예요.

You're right. If he continues to hang around with that group, he will eventually end up in jail.

[Note] hang around (근처를) 배회하다(loiter)/end up 결국에는 ~이 되다, 마침내 ~에 이르다

424 좌석이 없다
All the seats are taken, We don't have any seats available.

DIALOG 1
A : 창문 쪽의 좌석을 원합니다.
I'd like a seat by the window, please.
(혹은 I'd like to sit by the window.)

B : 미안합니다만 **좌석이 모두 찼습니다.**
I'm sorry, **they're all taken.**

DIALOG 2
A : 그 비행기에는 **좌석이 없습니다.** 다음 비행기로 가시겠어요?
I'm sorry, **we don't have any seats available** on that flight. Would you like to try a later flight?

B : 아무거나 좋아요. 두 시간 정도면 별로 문제가 안 되니까요.
Whatever. A couple hours won't make any difference.

[Note] 빈 좌석이 없어서 좀 더 기다려 봐야겠어요.
You have to go on stand-by since there are no seats available.

425 (꾸벅꾸벅) 졸다
doze off

DIALOG 1
A : 그 강의 참 재미있었어.
The lecture was very interesting.

B : 나는 그 말에 찬성 못해. 나는 지루했어. **계속 꾸벅꾸벅 졸기만 했는걸.**
I can't go along with that. I was bored. **I kept dozing off.**

[Note] go along with~ (의견 따위에) 찬성하다, 지지하다

DIALOG 2

A : 정말 피곤해서 영화 보러 가고 싶지 않아. 영화 보는 도중에 **꾸벅꾸벅 졸 거야.**

I'm really tired. I don't think I want to go to a movie.

I'd **doze off** in the middle of it.

B : 그러면 기숙사에서 돌아다닐 거니?

Then do you want to hang around the residence halls?

[Note] 그는 너무 피곤해 꾸벅꾸벅 졸면서 운전을 하고 있었다.

He was so tired that he was dozing off behind the wheel.

점심 식사 후에 잠깐 낮잠을 안 자면 일하면서 꾸벅꾸벅 졸게 된다.

If I don't take a little nap(snooze) after lunch, I doze off while working.

426 (더할 나위 없이) 좋은

Couldn't be better.

DIALOG

A : 헨리, 요즘 어떻게 지내니?

Henry, how are you these days?

B : 잘 지내. 넌 어때?

I'm getting by. How's everything with you?

A : **더할 나위 없이 좋아.**

Couldn't be better.

[Note] get by (어려움을 극복하고) 그럭저럭 헤쳐나가다

427 (더 이상) 좋을 수가 없다

You couldn't ask for better, It couldn't be better.

DIALOG 1

A : 그분 좋은 분이지요?

Is he a good person?

B : 오, 굉장히 좋은 분이지요. **더 이상 좋을 수가 없어요.**

Oh, terrific. **You couldn't ask for better.**

DIALOG 2

A : 날씨가 어때요?

How's the weather?

B : **더 이상 좋을 수가 없을 정도예요.**

It couldn't be better.

428 주문하시겠어요?

May I take your order?

DIALOG

A : **주문하시겠어요?**

May I take your order?

B : 감사합니다. 이미 주문했어요.

Thank you. I'm being waited on.

429 죽어지내다(쥐어 살다, 꼼짝 못하다)

live under one's thumb

DIALOG

A : 그는 부인과 어떻게 지내니?

How is he getting along with his wife?

B : **부인한테 죽어 지내지.**

He lives under his wife's thumb.

430 죽이 되든 밥이 되든

sink or swim

DIALOG

A : 아직도 그 일을 할 생각이니?

Are you still thinking of doing the work?

B : **죽이 되든 밥이 되든** 해 보겠어요.

Sink or swim, I'll try.

[Note] Starting a new job makes me feel like I'll sink or swim.

새로운 직업을 시작한다는 것은 흥하지 않으면 망하겠지 하는 느낌을 갖게 만든다.

431 줄을 서다

get in line

DIALOG

A : 줄이 너무 긴데요.

It's too long a line.

B : 하지만 새치기는 안 됩니다. **줄을 서야 해요.**

You shouldn't cut in ahead of other people. You must **get in line.**

[Note] cut in ahead of other people 다른 사람들 앞에 새치기하다

432 줄을 서서 기다리다

wait in line

DIALOG

A : 당신 차례가 아닙니다. 앞에 일곱 명이나 있어요. 새치기도 안 되고요.

It's not your turn. There are seven ahead of you. You shouldn't cut in ahead of them.

B : 그렇게 오래 **줄을 서서 기다려야 하나요**?

Do I really have to **wait** that long **in line**?

433 줄이다(비용, 옷, 음식 양, 담배 등)

cut down(on)

DIALOG

A : 사업이 불경기예요.

Business is very slow.

B : 사업을 계속하고 싶으면 **비용을 줄여야 해요**.

We'll have to **cut down our expenses** if we wish to continue in business.

434 중매로

through a matchmaker

DIALOG

A : 어떻게 부인과 결혼하게 되었나요?

How did you meet your wife?

B : 친구의 **중매로요**.

Through a friend, who is a real **matchmaker**.

[Note] A를 "How did you get married with your present wife?"라고 하지 말 것/matchmaker 중매인(= a go-between)

435 중퇴하다

drop out of school

DIALOG

A : 그는 아직도 대학에 다니니?

Is he still attending college?

B : 아니요, **중퇴했어요**.

No. He **dropped out of school**.

436 쥐고 흔들다

be bossy

DIALOG

A : **당신은 저를 너무 쥐고 흔들어요**. 이제 그만하세요. 저를 화나게 해요.

You're so bossy. Please stop telling me what to do. It makes me angry.

B : 당신을 위한 거예요.

It's for your sake.

[Note] 한국의 시어머니는 주로 며느리를 쥐고 흔들려고 한다.

In Korea the mother-in-law is usually very bossy.

"쥐고 흔들다"의 다른 표현은 "have a person under one's thumb"이다.

즉 Janet has her husband right under her thumb.

437 즉흥적으로

off the top of one's head

DIALOG

A : 그는 연설 준비를 잘 하지 않은 것 같아요.

I don't think he planned his speech very well.

B : 맞아요, 그는 **즉흥적으로** 연설을 했어요.

No, he was speaking **off the top of his head**.

438 (~의) 증거(기념)로, 증표로
as a token of

DIALOG

A : 당신에 대한 우정의 **증표로** 이것을 받아 주세요.
Please accept this **as a token of** my friendship for you.

B : 감사합니다. 우리가 평생 좋은 친구로 지내기를 바랍니다.
Thank you. I want us to be good friends for the rest of our lives.

439 지겨운 사람
a bore

DIALOG

A : 그는 내가 좋아하는 선생님이야.
He's my favorite teacher.

B : 농담도! 모두 그를 **지겨운 사람**이라고 생각하는데요.
You're kidding! Everyone thinks he's **a bore**.

440 지겨운 일
a pain in the neck

DIALOG

A : 눈이 너무 많이 와서 버스가 다니지 않았어요. 그래서 상점에서 집까지 걸어왔어요.
Because of the heavy snow, there were no buses running. I had to walk home from the store.

B : **정말 지겨운 일이었군요!**
That's a real pain in the neck!

441 지나간 일은 지나간 일로 덮어 두다
Let bygones be bygones.

DIALOG

A : 제가 사과할 일이 있어요. 어제 당신의 감정을 상하게 해 드린 것 같아요.
I owe you an apology. I think I hurt your feelings yesterday.

B : 잊어버리세요. **지나간 일은 지나간 일로 덮어 두자고요.**
Forget it. **Let bygones be bygones.**

442 지나치다 (심하다)
go too far

DIALOG

A : 사장에게 바보라고 했어요.
I told my boss he was stupid.

B : 당신이 너무 **지나쳤어요.**
I think **you went too far.**

[Note] 농담이 너무 지나치다. You carried your joke a little too far.

443 지루해서 죽을 지경이야
die of boredom

DIALOG

A : **지루해서 죽을 지경이에요.** 나는 활동적이거든요. 테니스를 치든 무엇이든. 비가 오는 게 싫어요.
I'm dying of boredom. I'm rather active–play tennis or something. I hate it when it rains.

B : 나는 안 그래요. 떨어지는 빗방울을 바라보는 것을 좋아해요.

Not me. I love to stare at the raindrops.

444 (~에) 지장이 없다

don't impair~

DIALOG

A : 괜찮으세요?

Are you all right?

B : 네, 맥주 한 잔 정도야 운전에 **지장이 없어요.**

Yes. One glass of beer **doesn't impair** my driving ability.

[Note] impair 해치다, 손상시키다, 약하게 하다

445 (정확하게) 지적하다

put one's finger on

DIALOG

A : 어떻게 오셨나요?

What brought you here?

B : **정확하게 지적은 못하지만** 저에게 이상이 있는 것 같아요. 요즘 입맛도 없고 쉽게 피곤해요.

I can't put my finger on it, but I'm afraid something must be wrong with me. I've lost my appetite and I get tired too easily these days.

A : 좋아요, 전반적인 진단을 해 봅시다.

All right. Let's have a general checkup.

446 지지하다

support, stand behind

DIALOG

A : 이번 선거에서 저를 **지지해** 주세요.

Will you **support** me in this election campaign?

B : 계속해서 **지지하겠습니다.**

I'll **stand behind** you all the way.

447 지출을 줄이다

cut down on one's expenses

DIALOG

A : 수입이 100달러, 지출이 120달러, 균형이 안 맞아요.

Income $ 100, expense $120. It doesn't balance.

B : **지출을 줄일** 방법이 없나요?

Don't you have any way to **cut down on our expenses**.

[Note] 수입과 지출 revenue and expendifure, income and outgo

448 직선거리(최단거리)로

as the crow flies, in a beeline

DIALOG

A : 그들 집과 당신의 집은 얼마나 떨어져 있나요?

How far is their house from yours?

B : **직선거리(최단거리)로** 10마일이지만 산을 둘러가야 하니까 훨씬 더 멀지요.

Their house is about ten miles from ours, **as the crow flies**; but of course the road is much longer since it winds around the mountains.

449 직선적이다

be direct, shoot from the hip

DIALOG

A : 그 사람 질문하는데 정말 **직선적이군요**.

He is certainly **direct** in his questioning.

B : 그는 항상 **직선적이라고** 하더군요.

They say he always **shoots from the hip.**

450 직업이 둘이다

wear two hats

DIALOG

A : 그가 6개월 만에 그렇게 많은 돈을 벌다니 믿어지지 않아요.

It's unbelievable to think he made so much money in six months.

B : **그가 두 개의 직업을 갖고 있다**면 가능한 일이지요.

It's a possibility if **he wore two hats**.

[Note] a possibility 가능한 일

451 직책을 맡다

fill the position

DIALOG

A : 당신은 그 **직책을 맡을** 자격이 있다고 생각하나요?

Do you think you have the qualifications to **fill the position**?

B : 네, 물론이죠.

Yes, I certainly do.

A : 그 자리에 대한 당신의 자격은 어떤 거죠?

What's your qualifications for the position?

452 진정하다

calm down, stay calm, simmer down, cool it

DIALOG 1

A : 너의 아버지께서 화가 많이 나셨어.

Your father has lost his temper.

B : **진정하시기**를 기다려야 할까요?

Shall I wait for him to **calm down**?

[Note] lose one's temper = become angry

DIALOG 2

A : 지금 저는 초조해졌어요.

I've got butterflies in my stomach.(I'm nervous.)

B : **진정하세요.**

Try to **stay calm.**

[Note] have butterflies in one's stomach 초조해하다

DIALOG 3

A : **진정하게**, 자네 성질이 급하군.

Simmer down. You sure have a hot (quick, short) temper, haven't you?

B : 그래서 어떻단 말인가? 자네하고는 끝장일세.

So what? I'm through with you!

453 진통을 시작하다

start labor pains

DIALOG

A : 저는 막 **진통을 시작했어요.**

I've just **started labor pains.**

B : 우선 진통제를 좀 드릴게요.

First I'll give you some tranquilizers.

454 질색이다

turn off

DIALOG

A : 음악 연주회에 함께 갈래요?

Why don't you join us at the concert?

B : 그러고 싶기는 하지만 저는 사람 많은 곳은 **질색이에요.**

I'd love to, but I'm really **turned off** by crowds.

455 질투가 심한

green with envy

DIALOG

A : 제 다이아몬드 반지 어때요?

How do you like my diamond ring?

B : 아름답군요. **몹시 질투가 나는데요.**

It's beautiful. **I'm green with envy.**

[Note] green 질투하는(jealous)/green-eyed 질투가 심한, 질투심이 많은

456 짐작하다

guess

DIALOG 1

A : 그의 나이가 얼마나 될까요?

How old do you think he is?

B : 겉으로 보아 스물은 된 것으로 **짐작이 되는군요**.

From his appearance I'd **guess** his age at 20.

DIALOG 2

A : 제 나이를 어떻게 알게 되었나요?

How did you know how old I was?

B : **그저 짐작이 맞은 거예요.**

Just a lucky guess.

457 집들이

housewarming

DIALOG

A : 새 집을 샀는데 **집들이는** 언제 해요?

I heard you've bought a new house.

When is the **housewarming**?

B : 다음 토요일 7시에요.

Next Saturday at 7 o'clock.

458 집을 보다

housesit

DIALOG

A : 제가 없는 동안 **집** 좀 **봐주시겠어요**?

Can you housesit while I'm away?

B : 얼마나 오래 있을 예정인데요?

How long will you be gone?

459 집에 틀어박혀 있다
be cooped up in the house

DIALOG

A : 이렇게 좋은 날씨에 **집에 틀어박혀 있다니요**. 자, 볼링이나 치러 갑시다.
Why are you **cooped up in the house** on a nice day like this? Come on, let's go bowling.

B : 좋아요. 오늘 당신 덕분에 신나는 날이었어요.
Oh, great. You made my day.

[Note] coop (닭 따위를 넣는) 둥우리, 우리, 비좁은 장소. I feel cooped up in this room. 이 방에 들어오면 우리에 갇힌 것 같은 기분이야./cooped up 좁은 장소에 갇힌. How can you work cooped up in this little office all day? 하루 종일 이 조그마한 방에 갇혀 어떻게 근무하니?

460 (그는) 집을 비우는 날이 많다
He's gone a lot.

DIALOG

A : **그는 집에 있는 날이 드물다.**
He's gone a lot.

B : 그럼 그의 부인은 집에 홀로 있는 날이 많겠군요.
Then his wife is often alone at home, isn't she?

차

461 차량이 밀려 꼼짝 못했다

Traffic was at a standstill.

DIALOG

A : 오늘 아침 고속도로에서 **차량이 밀려 꼼짝 못했어요.**

This morning **traffic was at a standstill** on the expressway.

B : 나는 다른 길로 왔더니 교통이 복잡하지 않았어요.

I took a different route, and the traffic was very light.

[Note] standstill 정지, 막힘

The work was at a standstill. 그 일은 정돈된 상태였다.

462 차례로 하다(교대로 하다)

take turns

DIALOG

A : 피곤하지 않았어요?

Weren't you tired?

B : 아니요, **교대로 운전해서** 여행이 피곤하지 않았어요.

No. Since we **took turns driving**, we didn't find the trip too tiring.

463 차를 앞으로 빼다

move up

DIALOG

A : 미안하지만 차를 조금만 **앞으로 빼주시겠어요**? 제 차가 가운데

끼어 나올 수가 없군요.

Excuse me. Could you **move up** a little, please? I'm kind of sandwiched between two cars and can't get out.

B : 그러지요.

No problem.

[Note] sandwich 끼워(틀어) 넣다/be sandwiched in between the two 두 사람 사이에 끼다

464 (의견 등에) 찬성하다

go along with

DIALOG

A : 테니스 치러 갑시다. 그러고 나서 시원한 맥주 한잔해요.

Let's go play tennis. After that, we can have some cold beer.

B : 좋지요. 그 의견에 **찬성입니다.**

Great. I'll **go along with** that idea.

465 (훗날) 참고가 될지 모르니

for the future reference

DIALOG

A : 당장 지금은 그에게 편지 쓸 시간이 없어요.

I have no time to write to him.

B : 혹시 훗날 **참고가** 될지 모르니 그의 주소를 알려 드릴게요.

I' ll tell you his address **for the future reference.**

466 (이를 악물고) 참다

grin and bear it

DIALOG

A : 나는 그와 같이 일하고 싶지 않아요.

I don't like working with him.

B : **참는 수밖에 없어요**. 그는 사장의 조카니까요.

You'll just have to **grin and bear it**. He's the boss's nephew.

[Note] grin and bear it (고통 · 억울함을) 이를 악물고 억지로 참다. grin(고통 · 노여움으로) 이를 악물다, 이를 악물며 벼르다.

467 참는 데도 한도가 있다

Enough is enough.

DIALOG 1

A : 이 형편없는 식사 좀 봐요. 이 기숙사 식사에 질렸어요.

Look at this lousy meal! **I'm fed up** with this dorm food.

B : 말씀 잘하셨어요. 나도 신물이 나요. 이제 **더 이상 못 참겠어요**.

You said it. I'm sick and tired of it, too. **Enough is enough**.

A : 지배인에게 좀 따집시다.

Let's **give the manager a piece of our mind**.

[Note] be fed up with~ ~에 질리다, 싫증나다. I'm fed up with your grumbling. 너의 불평에 질렸어./give someone a piece of one's mind (남에게) 자기 의견을 기탄없이 말하다, (남을) 호되게 꾸짖다.

DIALOG 2

A : 직장을 그만둘 작정이에요?

Are you going to quit your job?

B : 네, 이 직장은 **더 이상 못참겠어요**.

Yes. **I've had this job up to here**.

[Note] I've had it up to here. 참을 만큼 참았다, 더 이상 못 참겠다.

468 창피하다

hurt one's dignity

DIALOG 1

A : 돌에 걸려 넘어지셨군요. 다치지 않았나요?

You tripped over a stone. Didn't you get hurt?

B : 다치기보다는 **창피했어요.**

I **hurt my dignity** more than I hurt myself.

[Note] trip over~ 걸려 넘어지다(stumble)/hurt oneself 다치다, 부상입다(get hurt).

DIALOG 2

A : 그는 시험에 낙방했어요.

He failed the test.

B : 네, 알아요. 그것에 대해서 **창피해하고 있어요.**

Yes, I know. He's very **embarrassed** about it.

469 처리하다

handle, take care of

DIALOG

A : 그것을 도와드릴까요?

Why don't you let me help you with that?

B : 괜찮아요. 혼자서 **처리할 수 있어요.**

That's all right. I can **handle** it alone.

470 처방대로 약을 짓다

have a prescription filled

DIALOG

A : 이 **처방대로 약 좀 지어 주세요.**

I'd like to **have** this **prescription filled**.

B : 좋습니다. 재고가 있는지 볼게요.

All right. Let me see if we have it in stock.

471 처분하다

get rid of

DIALOG

A : 나는 차를 새로 사고 헌차는 **처분해야 해.**

I'm buying a new car and I have to **get rid of** my old car.

B : 얼마를 요구하는데?

How much are you asking?

472 처지가 같다

be in the same boat

DIALOG

A : 물가가 올라가는 요즘에 가난한 사람들은 간신히 살아가는 것도 어려운 일이야.

In these days of rising prices it is difficult for many poor people to keep body and soul together.

B : 이런 인플레 때 우리 노동자들은 모두 **같은 처지지요.**

We wage earners **are all in the same boat** during these inflationary times.

[Note] keep body and soul together 간신히 살아가다, 겨우 입에 풀칠하다

473 천성에 맞다

be cut out to be a~

DIALOG

A : 왜 축구하는 것을 포기했어요?

Why did you quit playing soccer?

B : 축구 선수가 **천성에 맞지 않아요**.

I'm **not cut out to be** a soccer player.

[Note] quit ~ing = give up ~img ~하는 것을 포기하다

474 천천히 걷다

slow down

DIALOG

A : 너무 빨라서 따라갈 수가 없어요. 좀 **천천히 가세요**.

You walk so fast that I can't catch up with you.

Why don't you **slow down**?

B : 7시에 늦지 않으려면 서둘러야 해요. 더 빨리 걸읍시다.

We have to hurry to make it by seven. Try to walk faster.

[Note] catch up with~ ~을 뒤따라 잡다(overtake)/slow down 속도를 줄이다 (reduce speed)

475 철이 없는

immature, wet behind the ears

DIALOG

A : 그는 아직 **철이 없어요.** 철이 좀 들어야 해요.

He's still **wet behind the ears.** He just needs to grow up.

B : 그래요. 그는 **철이 없어요.** 같이 어울리기가 무척 힘들어요.

You said it. He's very **immature.** He's very hard to get along with.

476 청소

cleaning

DIALOG

A : 오늘 당신 부지런하군요. 무슨 일로 이렇게 **청소까지** 했어요?

You're really industrious today. What prompted all this **cleaning**?

B : 봄이라서요. **청소하고 싶어서 좀이 쑤셔요.**

It's spring. **I've got the cleaning bug.**

[Note] industrious 열심히 일하는, 부지런한/prompt 남을 자극하다, 부추기다, 꼬드기다

477 체격이 좋다

have a nice (good) build, be in shape

DIALOG 1

A : 저 권투선수 **체격이 좋은데요.**

That fighter **has a nice physique(build).**

B : 네, 정말 **체격이 좋군요.**

Yes. **He's** really **in shape.**

DIALOG 2

A : 당신 형은 **체격이 좋습니다.**

Your brother **has a good build.**

B : 일주일에 세 번씩 운동을 합니다.

He works out three times a week.

478 체계적으로 하세요

get organized

DIALOG

A : 당신은 무엇이든 좀 **체계적으로 하세요.** 우선 무엇을 할 것인지 결정하고 다음에 그것을 하세요.

You just need to **get organized.** Decide what to do first and then do it.

B : 그래요?

Really?

A : 저는 그런 식으로 합니다.

That's my system.

479 체중이 늘다

put on(= gain) weight

DIALOG

A : 금년 겨울에 **체중이 몇 파운드 늘어났어요.**

I've **put on a few pounds** this winter.

B : 그러면 식이요법을 하지요?

Then why aren't you on a diet?

[Note] 체중이 줄다 lose weight

480 체중 조절을 하다

slim down

DIALOG

A : 캔디 먹을래?

Would you care for some candy?

B : 감사합니다만 **체중 조절을 해야 해요.**

No, thank you. I have to **slim down.**

[Note] care for~ ~을 좋아하다/slim (절식 · 운동 따위로) 체중을 줄이다

481 초봉이 얼마예요?

What is the starting salary?

DIALOG

A : **초봉이 얼마나 되는지** 여쭤 봐도 될까요?

May I ask **what the starting salary is**?

B : 기타 각종 혜택을 합쳐서 15,000달러예요.

About $15,000 plus fringe benefits.

[Note] fringe benefit (주택, 건강보험, 병가 따위의) 특별급여

482 (~하는 것이) 최고야

There's nothing like it. Couldn't be better

DIALOG

A : 테니스를 친 다음 피곤하면 어떻게 하나요?

What do you do when you are very tired after playing tennis?

B : 더운물에 목욕하고 시원한 맥주 한잔 하지요. **그게 최고지요.**

I take a hot bath and then drink a cold beer. **There's nothing like it!**

483 최저 가격입니다
It's a rock-bottom price.

DIALOG

A : 더 이상 깎아 줄 수 없나요?
Can't you knock down the price anymore?

B : 안 돼요. 그것이 **최저 가격이에요.**
No, I can't. **It's a rock-bottom price.**

484 축배를 들다
toast, drink a toast to

DIALOG

A : 결혼식은 굉장히 훌륭했어요.
This whole wedding has been splendid.

B : 저것 봐요! 사람들이 신혼부부에게 **축배를 들자고 하네요.**
Oh, look! They're about to **toast** the newlyweds.

[Note] splendid 훌륭한, 화려한, 웅장한, 장려한/newlyweds 신혼부부

485 몇 시에 출근하나요?
What are his hours?
What time does he report for work?

DIALOG

A : 김 선생님 좀 부탁합니다.
May I speak to Mr. Kim?

B : **아직 출근 전입니다.**
He's not in yet.

A : **몇 시에 출근하시나요?**

What time does he report for work?
(혹은 **What are his hours? What time does he punch in?**)

[Note] 출근하다 show up at the office 혹은 go to work(the office)
그는 출근이 불규칙하다. He's irregular in his attendance.

486 출입구가 따로 있다
have a private entrance

DIALOG
A : 그 집은 **출입구가 따로 있나요?**
Does the house **have a private entrance?**
B : 네. 방과 함께 부엌도 있어요.
Yes, it does. You also have kitchen privileges with the room.

487 춤을 못 추다
have two left feet

DIALOG
A : 나하고 춤을 추시겠어요?
Would you dance with me?
B : 미안합니다만 저는 **춤을 출 줄 몰라요.**
I'm sorry. I **have two left feet.**

[Note] I have two left feet = I'm not a good dancer

488 (정면) 충돌
head-on collision

DIALOG

A : 무서운 사고를 목격했어요. **정면충돌이었어요.**

I just witnessed a terrible accident. **It was a head-on collision.**

B : 모든 것을 다 보셨다는 말씀인가요?

You mean you really saw whole thing?

489 (눈이) 충혈되다

be bloodshot

DIALOG

A : 어쩌다 눈이 그렇게 되었어요? **눈이 충혈되었네요.**

What did you do to your eye? It's all **bloodshot.**

B : 테니스 공에 맞았어요

I got hit by a tennis ball.

490 (상품 등을) 취급하다

carry

DIALOG 1

A : 실크 타이 있나요?

Do you have silk ties?

B : 네, **취급합니다만** 오늘은 없군요.

We normally **carry** those, but we don't have them on hand today.

[Note] have ~on hand 갖추고 있다/We have some new goods on hand. 저희들은 신품을 갖추고 있습니다.

DIALOG 2

A : 이것은 일본 제품인가요?

Is this from Japan?

B : 우리는 일본 제품은 **취급하지 않아요.**

We **don't carry** goods from Japan.

491 (한 말을) 취소하다

take back

DIALOG

A : 나는 그가 좋은 사람이라고 생각했는데 그렇지 않아요.

I thought he was nice, but he isn't.

B : 나도 동감이야. 그에 대해 칭찬한 말들은 모두 **취소해야겠어.**

I agree. I **take back** all the nice things I ever said about him.

[Note] take back 취소하다, 철회하다(withdraw a statement)

492 취하다

tipsy

DIALOG

A : 왜 그렇게 일찍 자려고 해요?

Why are you going to bed so early?

B : 맥주 두 잔 했더니 약간 **취하는 것 같아요.**

I'm a little **tipsy** after two glasses of beer.

493 (몇) 층에 내리세요?

What floor do you want?

DIALOG 1

A : 몇 **층**에 내리세요?

What **floor** do you want?

B : 7층 좀 눌러 주세요.

Push seven, please.

DIALOG 2

A : 이곳이 내리실 **층**인가요?

Is this your **floor**?

B : 네, 실례합니다.

Yes. Excuse me, please.

DIALOG 3

A : **저는 여기에 내립니다**. 좀 나갑시다.

This is my floor. Out, please.

B : 저도 내립니다.

I'm getting off, too.

494 층계

flight of stairs

DIALOG

A : 왜 그렇게 피곤해 보여요?

Why are you so tired?

B : 엘리베이터가 고장나서 **5층까지** 걸어 올라왔어요.

As the elevator was out-of-order, I had to walk up **five flights of stairs**.

495 치근거리다

make passes(a pass) at

DIALOG

A : 그가 당신에게 늘 **치근거린다는** 생각이 들어요.

I think he's always **making passes** at you.

B : 네, 너무 치근거려서 더 이상 참을 수가 없어요.

Yes. I've had it up to here with his passes.

[Note] have had it 지겨워지다/up to here 더 이상 참을 수 없는 지경까지

496 치료약
remedy

DIALOG

A : 찰과상에 좋은 **치료약이** 뭐예요?

What's a good **remedy** for chafing?

B : 이 로숀이 좋습니다. 상처 부위에 바르기만 하세요.

This lotion is good for that. Just apply on the affected area.

[Note] chafing 살갗이 벗겨지기/affected 감염된

497 칭찬을 전해 주세요
My compliments to

DIALOG 1

A : 당신 요리사에게 **칭찬을 전해 주세요**. 모든 것이 완벽했고 음식도 훌륭했어요.

My compliments to your cook. Everything was perfect and the food was excellent.

B : 그렇게 하지요. 그녀는 의외로 잘했어요.

I'll tell her. She really outdid herself tonight.

[Note] outdo oneself 지금까지보다 더 잘 (열심히) 하다, 지금까지 이상의 성의를 표시하다, 의외로 잘하다(surpass expectation).

498 칭찬받고 우쭐하다

Compliment goes to one's head

DIALOG

A : 그는 약간만 **칭찬받아도 우쭐해요**.

One little **compliment** really **goes to his head**.

B : 아직 나이가 어려서 그래요.

It's because he's too young.

499 커피를 마시면서
over a cup of coffee

DIALOG

A : 김 교수님! 뜻밖에 만났군요!
Professor Kim! What a surprise!

B : 우리 어디 가서 **커피 마시면서** 이야기 좀 합시다.
Why don't we go somewhere and talk **over a cup of coffee**?

500 코가 막히다
have nasal congestion
have a stuffy nose

DIALOG 1

A : 무슨 냄새 나지 않아요? 나는 가스 냄새가 나는데요.
Don't you smell anything? I smell gas.

B : 아무 냄새도 못 맡아요. **코가 막혔어요.**
I can't smell a thing. I **have nasal congestion(a stuffy nose).**

[Note] stuffy (코가) 막힌, a stuffy nose 막힌 코

DIALOG 2

A : 설마 내 목소리를 잊었다고는 안하겠지.
Don't tell me you forget my voice.

B : 목소리가 좀 다른데. 감기 걸렸어요?
You sound a little different today. Have a cold or something?

A : **코가 약간 막혔어.**

Yeah, I **have a little nasal congestion.**

501 콧물이 나다
have a runny nose

DIALOG 1

A : 어디가 아픈가요?

What seems to be the problem?

B : **콧물이 납니다.**

I **have a runny nose.**

DIALOG 2

A : 독감 약 좀 주세요.

I'd like some medication for a bad cold.

B : 네. 증상이 어때요?

All right. What are your symptoms?

A : 온몸이 쑤시고 콧물이 나요.

I ache all over and have a runny nose.

[Note] symptom 징후, 증후, 징조

502 크레디트 카드를 사용하겠습니다
Charge it to my credit card.

DIALOG

A : 지불을 어떤 방식으로 하시겠어요?

How are you going to pay?

B : **비자 카드로 할게요.**

Charge it to my VISA Card.

503 크림을 많이 (조금) 넣으세요
Heavy on the cream(Just a touch).

DIALOG

A : 커피에 크림을 넣을까요?

Do you take cream in your coffee?

B : 네, **많이 넣어 주세요.**(혹은 조금만 넣어 주세요.)

Yes, **heavy on the cream**, please(or Just a touch, please.).

504 큰일 날 뻔했다.
That was a close call.

DIALOG

A : 저 사람 내 차를 받을 뻔했어.

That guy almost hit my car.

B : 그랬었지. 하마터면 **큰일 날 뻔했어.**

I'll say. **That was a close call.**

[Note] a close call 하마터면 큰일 날 뻔한 일, 구사일생(a close shave, a narrow escape)

타

505 타고난

natural, born

DIALOG

A : 그는 그 팀에서 없어서는 안 될 훌륭한 선수가 될 거라고 생각합니다.

I think he will make the team.

B : 저도 그렇게 생각해요. 그는 **타고난** 운동선수지요.

So do I. He's a **natural** athlete.

506 타이어가 구멍나다

The tire is flat.

DIALOG

A : 왜 그렇게 비참한 얼굴을 하고 있지?

Why do you look so helpless?

B : 타이어 갈아 끼는 법을 배우지 못했는데 **타이어가 구멍났어요**.

I've never learned how to change a tire, and now **it's flat**.

507 태연한 얼굴을 하다

keep a straight face

DIALOG

A : 나는 그녀와 결혼할 거야.

I'm going to marry her.

B : 자넨 그녀와 결혼할 수 없는 걸 알지 않나. 어떻게 그런 말을 하면서도 웃지 않고 **태연한 얼굴을 하고 있지**?

You know you won't. How can you **keep a straight face** when you say such things?

508 태워다 주다
give someone a lift(ride)

DIALOG

A : 왜 직장에 늦었어요?

Why were you late for work?

B : 한 친구를 직장에 **태워다 주느라** 늦었어요.

Because I **gave a friend a lift** to work.

509 (집, 가게 등을) 털다(~에 침입하다)
break into

DIALOG 1

A : 기분이 나빠 보이는데 무슨 일이야?

You look upset. What's wrong?

B : 지난밤 도둑이 **들어** 아내의 털코트를 훔쳐갔어.

Last night thieves **broke into** our apartment and stole my wife's fur coat.

DIALOG 2

A : 당신이 지난주에 가게를 **털린** 분이 아닌가요?

Aren't you the one whose store **was broken into** last week?

B : 네, 바로 접니다. 2,000달러 상당의 물건들을 훔쳐갔어요.

Yes. That's me. They took about $2,000 worth of merchandise.

510 테스트해 보다
try out

DIALOG 1

A : 어느 회사 차를 살 거예요?

Which make of car are you going to buy?

B : 최종 선택하기 전에 몇 종을 **테스트해** 볼 계획이에요.

I plan to **try out** several before making a final choice.

[Note] B의 대답에서 several makes of cars라고 할 필요가 없다. 단지 several만으로 훌륭하다.

DIALOG 2

A : 연극 **테스트는** 언제예요?

When are **the try-outs** for the play?

B : 오늘 저녁이에요.

Tonight.

511 통성명하다

meet

DIALOG

A : 우리는 한 시간 동안 이야기를 했는데 **아직 서로 이름을 모르고 있군요.(아직 통성명하지 않았군요.)**

We have been talking for about an hour, but **we haven't met yet**, have we?

B : 그렇군요. 제 이름은 헬렌이에요.

No. My name is Helen.

A : 저는 존이에요. 만나서 반갑군요.

I'm John. Nice to meet you.

B : 저도 그래요.

Same here.

[Note] I'm John 대신에 John here를 쓰기도 하는데 영국식 영어같이 들린다.

512 통증이 가시지 않는다

The pain is still persistent.

DIALOG

A : **아직 통증이 가시지 않아.** 어느 것도 통증을 없애 주지 못할 것 같아요.

The pain is still persistent. Nothing seems to relieve it.

B : 나는 치료법을 갖고 있어, 이 약을 먹으면 틀림없이 통증이 없어질 거야.

I have just the cure for you. This new drug will relieve the pain for sure.

513 통화중이다

be on another line

DIALOG 1

A : 김 교수님 좀 바꿔 주세요?

Can I speak to Professor Kim?

B : 지금 **통화중이신데,** 기다리시겠어요, 다시 거시겠어요?

He's on another line right now. Will you hold on or call back?

A : 기다리겠어요.

I'll hang on.

[Note] hang up 전화를 끊다/Only courtesy kept me from hanging up. 예의란 것에 구애되지 않았다면 중도에 전화를 끊었을 텐데.

DIALOG 2

A : 그는 지금 **통화 중인데** 무슨 용건인가요?

He's on another line right now. May I ask what this is regarding?

B : 개인적인 거예요.

It's personal.

A : 좋아요. 통화가 끝나는 대로 연결해 드릴 테니 끊지 말고 계세요.

All right. I'll connect you with him as soon as he is available. Hold the line, please.

[Note] regarding ~에 관한, ~에 대하여

514 퇴근하다

get off work

DIALOG 1

A : 러시아워는 5시부터 7시까지예요.

Rush hour is usually from five to seven in the afternoon.

B : 그 시간이 직장에서 모두 **퇴근하는** 시간이군요.

That's when everyone **gets off work**.

A : 그래요. 그때쯤 되면 교통이 항상 혼잡하지요.

Right. Traffic is always bumper to bumper.

DIALOG 2

A : 좀 일찍 **퇴근해도** 될까요?

Can I **be excused** a little early today?

B : 사장 말에 의하면 오늘 아무도 일찍 퇴근할 수 없다던데요.

According to the boss, no one can get off early today.

515 퇴원하다

be discharged from the hospital

be released from the hospital

DIALOG 1

A : 부인은 좀 어떠세요?

How's your wife doing?

B : 회복이 빨라 며칠 후면 **퇴원할 거예요**.

She's recovered quite well and **will be released** in a few days.

DIALOG 2

A : 언제 그가 **퇴원할 것 같은가요**?

When do you think he'll **be released from the hospital**?

B : 3일 후면 **퇴원할 거예요**.

He'll be discharged in three days.

[Note] be hospitalized 입원하다

516 틀튼하게 하다

build up, strengthen

DIALOG

A : 조깅하는 것이 뭐 그렇게 좋은가요?

What's so great about jogging anyway?

B : 심장과 폐기능을 **좋게 (튼튼하게) 해 주지요**.

It builds up your heart and lungs.

파

517 파산하다

go bankrupt, go out of business

DIALOG

A : 그 가게 아직도 영업하고 있나요?

Is the store still in business?

B : **파산했다고** 생각해요.

I think **it went out of business.**(or **it is no longer in business** or **it went bankrupt**)

518 팔자예요

That's just one's luck.

DIALOG

A : 왜 그와 이혼하지 않아요?

Why don't you divorce him?

B : 애당초 그와 결혼한 것이 다 **팔자지요.**

It was just my luck to marry him in the first place.

519 패자

loser

DIALOG

A : 자네하고 다시는 놀이를 안할 거야. 늘 내가 지는걸.

I don't want to play with you again. You always win.

B : 그렇게 **비열한 패자**가 되지 말아요.

Don't be such **a sore loser.**

520 퍼머하다

give someone a permanent

DIALOG

A : 오늘 **퍼머를 해 주실 수 있나요**?

Could you **give me a permanent** today?

B : 약속을 하지 않았으면 오늘 오후까지는 빈 시간이 없네요.

If you have no appointment with us, we have no openings until this afternoon.

521 편견을 갖다

have a prejudice(against)

be prejudiced

DIALOG

A : 편견은 자신을 망칠 수도 있어.

Prejudice can destroy yourself.

B : **나는 편견이 없어요**. 난 당신보다 친구가 더 많은걸요.

I'm not prejudiced. I've got more friends than you have.

[Note] 그는 외국인에 대해 편견을 가지고 있다. He has a prejudice against foreigners.

522 편리하다(쓸모가 있다)

come in handy

DIALOG

A : 아이스박스를 어디에 쓰려고 사나요?

What do you buy the cooler for?

B : 캠핑할 때 참 **편리해요**.

It **comes in handy** while we are camping.

523 편리한 곳에 두다
keep~ handy

DIALOG

A : 실수로 열쇠를 집 안에 두고 문을 잠가 버렸어요.
I accidentally locked myself out of the house.

B : 걱정 마세요. 저는 항상 여분의 열쇠를 편리한 곳에 두지요.
Don't worry. I always keep an extra key handy.

[Note] handy 솜씨있는, 능란한/you're handy with a needle. 바느질 솜씨가 좋다. I keep a dictionary handy. 사전을 곁에 준비해 둔다.

524 편리한 대로 하다
Suit yourself.

DIALOG

A : 오후 2시 대신 오전 11시에 만날 수 있을까요? 우리가 만난 다음 회의가 있어요.
Could we meet at eleven in the morning instead of at two in the afternoon? I have a conference to attend after our meeting.

B : 문제없어요. **편리하신 대로 하세요.**
No problem. **Suit yourself.**

A : 감사합니다. 불편하게 해 드린 건 아닌지요.
Thank you. I hope I'm not inconveniencing you.

[Note] inconvenience 불편, 폐. ~에게 불편을 느끼게 하다, 폐를 끼치다.

525 편리한 시간에
at one's convenience

DIALOG

A : 몇 시가 가장 적당한가요?

What time suits you best?

B : 오후에는 다른 약속을 하지 않을 테니 **편리한 시간에** 들르세요.

I will leave all afternoon open for you. So drop in **at your convenience**.

[Note] leave all afternoon open 오후에는 다른 약속을 하지 않고 비워 두다./drop in 잠깐 들르다(stop by). Mr. and Mrs. Johnes dropped in to see us last night on their way home from the movie. 존슨 씨 부부가 어제 저녁 영화를 보고 집으로 가는 도중에 우리를 만나러 잠깐 들렀다.

526 편들다
take one's side, take sides with~

DIALOG 1

A : 당신은 왜 그에게 반대하고 **내 편을 들었어요**?

Why did you **take my side** against him?

B : 당신 의견에 동의하니까요.

Because I agree with you.

DIALOG 2

A : 그 문제에 있어서 누구를 지지하나요?

Who do you support in that matter?

B : 저는 헨리 **편을 들고** 싶은데요.

I'm inclined to **side with** Henry.

[Note] Despite my friendship with Frank, I tried not to take sides with him in his argument with his brother. 나는 프랭크와 친구 사이지만 그와 그의 동생과 논쟁에서 그의 편을 들지 않도록 애썼다. side with ~에 편들다, (논쟁 따위에서) 지지하다

527 폐를 끼치다
put one to the bother

DIALOG

A : 제가 무가당 오렌지 주스를 사 드릴게요.
I'll buy you sugar-free orange juice.

B : 당신에게 **폐를 끼치고** 싶지 않아요.
I don't want to **put you to the bother**.

528 포기하다
give up, pass up

DIALOG

A : 나는 그런 직장은 싫어요.
I don't want such a job.

B : 어떻게 그런 좋은 기회를 **포기할 수 있어요**?
How could you **pass up** such an opportunity?

[Note] It was a good offer, and Bill naturally didn't feel like passing it up. 그것은 좋은 기회였으니 빌이 포기하고 싶지 않았던 것은 당연하다.

529 (선물을) 포장하다
gift-wrap

DIALOG

A : **선물 포장하는** 곳이 어디에요?

Where can **I have this gift-wrapped**?

B : 좋으시다면 제가 여기서 해 드리지요. 어디에 쓰실 건가요?

I can do it right here if you'd like. What's the occasion?

A : 제 아내의 생일이에요.

It's my wife's birthday.

[Note] "어디에 쓰실 건가요?"는 "어느 경우이냐?"의 뜻으로 "What's the occasion?" occasion은 (특수한) 경우, 즉 결혼, 약혼, 생일 등 어느 경우냐는 것.

530 (~의) 피가 흐르다

run in the family, be inherited

DIALOG

A : 존슨 집안 사람들은 모두 노래를 잘 해요.

All those Johnes sing so well.

B : **그 가족에게** 음악적인 재능의 **피가 흐르고 있다고 해요**.

They say that musical talent **runs in his family**.

[Note] 그들은 타고난 음악가들이다. They're born musicians.

531 핑계를 대다

make an excuse

DIALOG

A : 그보다 **더 그럴듯한 핑계를 둘러대야 해요**.

You'd better **make a better excuse** than that.

B : 이봐요! 나는 진실을 말하고 있는 거예요.

Look! I'm telling you the truth.

[Note] 핑계 말고 모임에 출석하라. Come to the meeting without making any excuses.

하

532 하고 싶은 대로 하다
have one's own way

DIALOG

A : 그 애 어떠니?
What do you think about him?

B : 그 애는 **하자는 대로 내버려 두었기** 때문에 말썽꾸러기야.
He is rather spoiled because his mother has always **let him have his own way**.

533 (당신 덕분에 신나는) 하루가 되다
You made my day!

DIALOG

A : 이렇게 좋은 날 집에 틀어박혀 있다니. 어서 볼링이나 치러 가요.
Cooped up in the house on a nice day like this. Come on, let's go bowling.

B : 야, 근사한데. 오늘은 **당신 덕분에 신나는 하루였어요**.
Oh, great. **You made my day**!

[Note] coop up = enclose in a small place/How can you work cooped up in that little office all day long? 하루 종일 그 자그마한 사무실에 갇혀서 어떻게 일을 하니?

534 (지루한) 하루
a long day

DIALOG

A : 여보, 오늘 어떻게 지냈어요?

How was your day, dear?

B : **지루한 하루였어요**. 제대로 되는 게 없었어요.

Well, **I had a long day**. Nothing went right.

535 (스타는) 하루 아침에 만들어지는 것이 아니다

Stars are not made overnight.

DIALOG

A : 내 동생은 돈을 쥐꼬리만큼 버는 별 볼 일 없는 배우야.

My kid brother is one of those small potatoes making chicken feed.

B : 글쎄, **스타는 하루 아침에 만들어지는 게 아니지.**

Well, **stars are not made overnight**.

536 하마터면 큰일 날 뻔했다

It was a close call.

DIALOG 1

A : 저 친구 정신 나갔군. 버스가 너무 가까이 와서 저 사람을 칠 뻔했어요.

That guy is crazy. Did you see how close that bus came to hitting that man?

B : 맞아요. **하마터면 큰일 날 뻔했어요.**

I agree. **That was a close call.**

A : 1인치만 더 가까웠더라도 저 사람은 죽었을 거야.

Another inch and that man would be dead.

DIALOG 2

A : 기차를 놓칠 뻔했어요. 자명종 시계가 울리지 않아서 아침도 못 먹고 역으로 달려야 했어요.

I almost missed my train. My alarm clock didn't go off.

I had to skip breakfast and run to the train station.

B : **하마터면 큰일 날 뻔했네요.**

That was a close call.

537 한 모금 마시다

take a sip

DIALOG

A : 네 커피 **한 모금 마셔도** 되니?

Can I **take (have) a sip** of your coffee?

B : 여기 있어요. 다 마셔도 돼요.

Here. You can have the whole cup.

538 한물가다

be over the hill

DIALOG

A : 그는 **한물간** 시대에 뒤떨어진 사람이야.

He is **over the hill** and behind the times.

B : 도전자의 나이를 악용하지 마세요.

Please don't take advantage of your challenger's age.

[Note] 그는 한창때가 지났다. He is past the prime of life.

그는 한창 일할 나이다. He is just in the prime of life.

539 한마디 따끔하게 해 주다

give a piece of one's mind

DIALOG

A : 그녀가 계속해서 나를 중상한다는데.

I hear that she continues to slander me.

B : 언제 한번 **따끔하게 한마디 하세요.**

Why don't you **give** her **a piece of your mind** some day?

[Note] slander 중상, 비방, 허위선전, (vt) 중상하다, (~의) 명예를 훼손하다.

540 (운에 맡기고) 한번 해 보다

take a chance

DIALOG

A : 어서 숫자를 하나 골라 상품을 타세요.

Hurry! Pick a number and win a prize.

B : **운에 맡기고 한번 해 보세요.**

Why don't you **take a chance**?

541 한번 해 보다(시도하다)

give it a try

DIALOG

A : 차 시동을 걸 수가 없어요.

I can't seem to get my car started.

B : 내가 **한번 해 봐도** 되겠어요?

Do you mind if I **give it a try**?

542 한수 높다

a cut above

DIALOG

A : 그 게임 결과가 어떻게 되었어요?

How did the game turn out?

B : 김 선생님이 이겼어요. 그는 상대방보다 **한수 높았어요.**

Mr. Kim won. He was **a cut above** his opponent.

[Note] 훨씬 위다(뛰어나다) head and shoulders above/As a salesman he is head and shoulders above any other man in our organization. 세일즈맨으로는 우리 회사에서 그를 따라갈 만한 사람이 없다.

543 한입 먹다

take a bite

DIALOG

A : 스테이크 냄새가 근사한데. **한입 먹어도 될까**?

That steak smells good. **Can I have a bite**?

B : 물론이지.

Sure.

544 한잔 더 주세요

I'd like a refill.

DIALOG

A : 커피 **한잔 더 할래요**?

Would you care for a refill?(another cup of coffee)

B : 네, **한잔 더** 주세요.

Yes, **a refill**, please.

A : 미안하지만 **한잔 더 부탁합니다.**

Excuse me, but **I'd like a refill**, please.

B : 여기 **한잔 더** 있습니다.

Refill coming up.

[Note] a refill 대신에 a warm up을 사용하는 사람도 있으나 a warm up보다는 a refill을 사용하는 것이 좋다.

545 한잔하다

drink to

DIALOG

A : 그가 과장으로 승진했어요

He was promoted to a section chief.

B : 그런 의미에서 **한잔 합시다.**

Let's drink to that.

546 한창이다

be in the prime of life

DIALOG

A : 그는 한물간 것 같아요.

It seems that he is over the hill.

B : 아니요, 저는 그가 지금 **한창때라고** 생각해요.

No, I think he **is in the prime of life.**

547 (당신들은 항상) 한편이다

You always stick together.

DIALOG

A : 저는 김 교수님 말씀에 동의해야겠는데요.

I'm afraid I have to agree with Professor Kim.

B : 뭐라고요? 당신도 그와 한편이군요. **당신들은 항상 한편이네요.**

What? You're taking his side, too? You men! **You always stick together.**

548 함정

catch

DIALOG

A : 보세요, 제주 왕복 여행에 단돈 3만 원이라고 하잖아요.

Let's see. It says that there is a round-trip tour to Jeju for only 30,000 won.

B : **함정이 있음에** 틀림없어.

There must be some **catch** to it.

[Note] catch (남을 옭아매는) 함정, 책략/There is some catch in your question. 자네 질문에는 함정이 있군.

549 해고하다

lay off

DIALOG

A : 나는 **해고당한** 지 3개월이 되었어요.

I have been laid off for three months.

B : 다른 직장을 찾고 있나요?

Are you looking for some other job?

[Note] lay off (불경기 때 일시적으로) 해고하다(dismiss workers during a slack period)/A sudden slump in business caused many of the plants to lay off workers. 갑작스런 사업 부진으로 많은 공장들이 근로자들을 해고시켰다.

550 해 보세요
Be my guest.

DIALOG 1

A : 왜 그것을 옳게 하지 못하나요?
Why can't you do it right?

B : **해 보세요**. 어떻게 하는지 보고 싶군요.
Be my guest. I want to see how you do it.

DIALOG 2

A : 아이들도 별로 어렵지 않게 할 수 있어요.
Any child could do it without too much difficulty.

B : **해 보세요**. 그것을 증명할 수 있는 기회군요.
Be my guest. Here is a chance for you to prove it.

551 행선지가 어딘가요?
Where are you headed?

DIALOG 1

A : 한국에서 **행선지가 어딘가요**?
What's your destination here in Korea?

B : 서울 그리고 다음엔 제주.
Seoul and then on to Jeju.

DIALOG 2

A : **행선지가 어딘가요**?(어디까지 가시나요?)
Where are you headed?

B : 부산까지 갑니다.

I go as far as Busan.

[Note] be headed for~(= head for~) ~쪽으로 향하다/I'm headed for Busan. 저는 부산까지 갑니다.

552 행실이 나쁘다
misbehave

DIALOG

A : 왜 그 아이의 엉덩이를 때렸어요? 말을 잘 안 들었나요?

Why did you spank him? Was he bad?

B : 네, **행실이 나빴어요**.

Yes, he **misbehaved**.

553 행운을 빌다
keep one's fingers crossed

DIALOG 1

A : 그에게 아무 일도 일어나지 않을 것을 확신합니다.

I'm sure that nothing will happen to him.

B : 하지만 **행운을 비는 것이** 좋겠어요.

But we'd better **keep our fingers crossed**.

DIALOG 2

A : 내일 중간고사가 있어요.

We're having our mid-term tomorrow.

B : **행운을 비네**.

I wish you the best of luck.(= I will keep my fingers crossed for you.)

554 행운의 여신이 축복해 주다
Lady luck does bless me.

DIALOG

A : 오늘 저녁 당신은 계속 운이 따르는군요.
You've been having a real winning streak tonight.
B : 가끔 **행운의 여신이** 저를 **축복해** 주지요.
Lady luck does occasionally **bless me with her presence**.

[Note] a winning streak 연속적인 승리, 연승

555 행운에 감사하다
thank one's lucky stars

DIALOG

A : 내가 어제 타기로 했던 비행기가 바다에 떨어졌어.
The plane I was supposed to take yesterday crashed into the sea.
B : 네가 그 비행기를 타지 않은 그 **행운에 감사해야 해.**
You can **thank your lucky stars** that you weren't on that plane.

556 잘했다
That's the way to go.

DIALOG

A : 모두 A를 받았어요.
I got all A's on my report card.
B : **잘했다.**("당연히 그렇게 해야 하지"의 뜻)
That's the way to go.

557 향상의 여지

room for improvement

DIALOG 1

A : 나는 건강한데 왜 운동을 해야 하나요?

I'm healthy. Why should I exercise?

B : 늘 **향상할 여지**는 있는 겁니다.

There's always **room for improvement**.

DIALOG 2

A : 자네 성적이 좋은데, 왜 그렇게 열심히 공부해야 하지?

Your grades are all right. Why should you study so hard?

B : 항상 **향상의 여지**는 있는 겁니다.

There's always **room for improvement**.

558 허풍떨다

brag

DIALOG

A : 그는 부자 아저씨를 가졌다고 **자랑해요**.

He **bragged** that he had a rich uncle.

B : 그는 항상 **허풍만 떤다**.

He's always **full of brag**.

[Note] brag 자랑(하다), 허풍(떨다)

559 헛걸음하다

make a trip for nothing

DIALOG

A : 당신 사진이 다 준비되어 있는 것 같아요.

I think your pictures are ready to go.

B : 다시 한번 확인해 주세요. **헛걸음하고** 싶지 않으니까요.

Will you double-check, please? I don't want to **make a trip for nothing**.

[Note] double-check 재확인하다/make a trip for nothing에서 for nothing 대신 in vain (헛되이) ~을 사용해도 좋다

560 헛수고가 되다(수포로 돌아가다)
be down the drain

DIALOG

A : 당신의 제의는 실행 가능성이 없어요.

Your proposal lacks feasibility.

B : 한 달 내내 일한 것이 **헛수고란 말씀이에요**?

You mean that a whole month's hard work is **down the drain**.

[Note] feasible 실행할 수 있는, 실행 가능한. feasibility 실행 가능성

561 (교제하다가) 헤어지다
break up

DIALOG 1

A : 내 남편은 아직도 사무실 여자와 어울려 다녀요.

My husband is still running around with a girl from the office.

B : 그 사람들 **헤어졌다고** 했잖아요?

Didn't you say they **had broken up**?

A : 그가 나에게 거짓말했어요.

He lied to me.

DIALOG 2

A : 당신은 왜 여자 친구와 **헤어지려고** 하나요?

Why are you **breaking up** with your girl friend?

B : 행동이 안 좋아요. 사람들 앞에서 나에게 소리도 지르고 말도 요란스럽게 하거든요.

Because her actions are in bad taste; she yells at me and talks too loudly in public.

[Note] be in bad taste 행동의 격이 낮다

562 혀 끝에 뱅뱅 돌다
on the tip of one's tongue

DIALOG

A : 그의 이름이 뭐죠?

What's his name?

B : **혀 끝에 뱅뱅 도는데** 도무지 기억이 안 나요.

It's **on the tip of my tongue**, but for the life of me I can't remember it.

A : 괜찮아요. 나중에 생각나겠지요.

That's okay. It'll come to you later.

563 호되게 꾸짖다(따끔하게 한마디 하다)
give one a piece of one's mind

DIALOG

A : 그 애는 지저분해요.

She is messy.

B : 돌아오면 제가 **호되게 꾸짖을게요.**

When she gets back, I'm going to **give her a piece of my mind.**

A : 그냥 둬요. 제가 치우지요.

Just let it go. I'll clean it up.

564 혹 떼러 갔다 혹 붙여 오다

get rid of trouble and end up with twice as much

DIALOG

A : 그에게 도움을 요청하지 않는 편이 더 나을 거야.

You'd better not ask for his help.

B : 동감이야. **혹 떼러 갔다 혹 붙여 오는 격이** 될지 몰라.

I agree. I'm afraid I try to **get rid of trouble and end up with twice as much.**

[Note] end up with~ 결국 ~신세가 되다/twice as much 두 배의 양

565 혹시나

by any chance

DIALOG 1

A : **혹시** 오늘 오후 시간 좀 있어요?

By any chance, are you free this afternoon?

B : 네, 시간이 있습니다.

Yes, I am.

DIALOG 2

A : **혹시** 몇 시인가요?

By any chance, do you have the time?

B : 네, 3시입니다.

Yes. It's 3 o'clock.

DIALOG 3

A : **혹시** 지금 세 사람 앉을 테이블 있나요?

Do you **by any chance** have a table for three available right now?

B : 지금 당장은 없지만 몇 분 후면 하나 날 거예요. 기다리겠어요?

Not right now, but a table will be available in a few minutes. Would you like to wait?

A : 물론이죠. 요행을 바라고 들어오길 잘했군.

Sure. I'm glad I took a chance.

[Note] take a chance 요행을 바라고 해 보다

566 혼동하다

mix up

DIALOG 1

A : 우리 약속이 내일 금요일이지.

Our appointment is for tomorrow, Friday.

B : 아니, 어제 수요일이었어

No, it was yesterday, Wednesday.

A : 그래, 네 말이 맞아. 날짜를 **혼동했어**.

Oh, you're right. I'm all **mixed up** on the day.

DIALOG 2

A : 그들의 이름이 **혼동되는군**.

I get **mixed up** with their names.

B : 외우기만 하면 되는 거야.

You simply have to memorize them.

A : 알아. 하지만 어쩐지 머릿속에 정리할 수가 없어.

I know, but for some reason, I just can't keep them straight in my mind.

[Note] 선생님은 항상 나를 이름이 같은 다른 학생과 혼동하신다.

The teacher always mixes me up with another student of the same name.

567 혼자만 알고 있다(비밀로 하다)

keep to oneself

DIALOG

A : 그건 **혼자만 알고 있었으면 좋겠어요.**

I want you to **keep** it **to yourself.**

B : 알았어요. 그런데 왜 **비밀로 하고 싶은 거죠**?

Oh, all right. Why do you want to **keep it a secret**?

568 화를 내다(노발대발하다)

hit the ceiling

DIALOG

A : 네가 아버지 차를 완전히 망가뜨려 놓은 것을 알고 화를 내시던가?

Did your father get angry when he knew you had totaled his car?

B : 화를 내시더냐구요? 말씀 마세요. **노발대발하셨어요.**

Get angry? Boy, **he hit the ceiling.**

[Note] total 완전히 망가뜨리다, 박살을 내다

569 화장하다

put on one's make-up, wear make-up

DIALOG 1

A : 거기서 뭐해?

What are you doing there?

B : **화장하고 있어.**

I'm putting on my make-up.

DIALOG 2

A : 그 여자는 왜 그렇게 **조잡하게 화장을 하고 있니**?

Why is she **wearing such trashy make-up**?

B : 그것이 새로운 유행이거나 일시적인 유행인 것 같아요.

I think it's a new fashion or fad.

570 화초를 잘 가꾸다

have a green thumb

DIALOG

A : 제 취미는 정원 가꾸기예요.

My hobby is gardening.

B : 당신의 집 식물들은 아름답게 자라고 있군요. **화초 가꾸는 솜씨가 대단한** 것 같아요.

All your house plants grow beautifully. You seem to **have a green thumb.**

571 화해하다

make up

DIALOG 1

A : 그가 부인하고 헤어졌다는 소식 들었어요?

Did you hear that he broke up with his wife?

B : 또? 걱정 마세요. 곧 **화해할 거예요**. 전에도 헤어졌다가 **화해한 적이 있어요**.

Again? Don't worry. They will **make up** pretty soon. They broke up and **made up** before.

DIALOG 2

A : 그 사람하고 **화해하시죠**.

Why don't you **make up** with him?

B : 나는 그 사람이 나를 사람 취급하지 않는 것에 진저리가 나요.

I'm tired of being put down like I'm nobody.

[Note] put down 경멸(멸시)하다, 창피를 주다 / nobody (특히 사회적으로) 보잘것없는 사람, 하찮은 사람(insignificant person)

DIALOG 3

A : 네가 친구와 **화해한** 줄로 생각했어.

I thought you **made up** with your friend.

B : 아니, 그가 내게 사과를 해야 해.

No. He still owes me an apology.

[Note] owe me an apology "나에게 사과를 해야 한다"는 뜻.

572 확신하다

feel (be) confident(sure)

DIALOG

A : 당신은 그것을 올바르게 했다고 **확신하나요**?

Are you confident you did it right?

B : **더 이상 확신할 수 없을 정도예요.**

I couldn't be more sure.

[Note] 우리 팀이 이길 것을 확신한다. I feel confident that our team will win.

573 확정되다

be all set, be definite

DIALOG

A : 당신의 겨울 휴가 계획이 다 **확정되었다고** 생각했어요.

I thought your plans for winter vacation **were all set.**

B : 아니, 모든 것이 아직 미정이에요.

No. Everything's still up in the air.

[Note] up in the air 미정이다(undecided ; not definite)/나의 계획은 아직도 확정되지 않았어요. My plans aren't definite yet.

574 환불하다

refund

DIALOG 1

A : 영수증을 가지고 와야 한다고 하셨나요?

Did you say I have to have the receipt?

B : 그렇습니다. 그것 없이는 **환불해** 드릴 수가 없어요.

That's what I said. Without it, we can't give you **a refund.**

DIALOG 2

A : 이 코트 환불해 주세요. 바느질이 엉망이고 산 지 2주밖에 안 되었는데 떨어지고 있어요.

I want my money back on this coat. The workmanship was terrible. I bought it exactly two weeks ago and it's falling apart.

B : 미안합니다만, 팔면 **환불은** 안 됩니다.

I'm sorry, but all sales are final and no **refunds**.

[Note] workmanship (직공들의) 솜씨, 세공 솜씨/fall apart 떨어지다, 낡아지다

575 회진 돌다
make a round

DIALOG

A : 김 박사님을 마이크로 불러 주시겠어요?

Would you please page Doctor Kim?

B : 안 됩니다. 지금 **회진을 돌고 있어요**.

No. **He's making his rounds**.

576 효과가 있다
do (work, perform) wonders

DIALOG 1

A : 좋아 보여요.

You look good.

B : 감사합니다. 식이요법의 **효력이 있군요**.

Thanks. My diet **has done wonders** for me.

DIALOG 2

A : 새 지배인이 이 가게를 훌륭하게 해 놓았어요.

The new manager has done wonders for this store.

B : 그래요. 여기서 물건 사는 것이 즐거워요.

I agree. It's pleasant to shop in here.

[Note] do (work) wonders 기적을 행하다, 놀랄 만큼 잘 되어 가다, (약 따위가) 놀랄 만큼 잘 듣다, 효과가 있다.

577 후식 먹을 자리를 남겨 두다
save room for dessert

DIALOG

A : **후식 먹을 자리를 남겨 뒀야 했어요.**
You should have saved room for dessert.

B : 항상 **후식 들어갈 자리는 남아 있어요.** 파이 한 조각 먹지요.
I always **have room for dessert.** Let me have a piece of pie.

578 휘발유를 가득 넣다
gas up, fill up

DIALOG

A : 저 주유소에 차를 세웁시다.
We'd better pull up at that filling station.

B : 휘발유가 떨어져 가나요?
Are we running out of gas?

A : 아니요, 하지만 오랜 여행하려면 **휘발유를 가득 넣는 것이** 좋겠지요.
No, but we'd better **gas up** for the long trip.

[Note] pull up (차 따위를) 세우다/run out of~ ~이 다 떨어지다/gas up 차에 휘발유를 가득 채우다(fill up a car tank with gasoline)

579 휴대용 짐
carry-on

DIALOG

A : **휴대용 짐이** 몇 개까지 허용되나요?

How many **carry-ons** am I allowed?

B : 좌석 밑에 들어갈 수 있는 것으로 단 한 개만 허용됩니다.

You're allowed only one carry-on which has to fit under the seat.

580 흔해 빠진 것들

a dime a dozen

DIALOG

A : 그는 배우인 것을 자랑으로 여기지요.

He is proud of being an actor.

B : **흔해 빠진 것이** 배우들인데 뭐.

Actors are a **dime a dozen**.

581 흠만 찾는(비판적인)

critical, faultfinding

DIALOG

A : 그는 내 옷에 **흠만 찾아요**.

He **finds fault with** my clothes.

B : 그는 매우 **비판적인** 사람이지요?

He's very **critical**, isn't he?

582 흥을 깨다

spoil the fun, cast a chill over, be a wet blanket

DIALOG

A : 왜 **흥을 깰** 결심을 했나요?

Why did you decide to **spoil the fun**?

B : 그럴 의도는 전혀 없었습니다.

I never had any intention of doing such a thing.

583 흥분하다

be excited, get[be] carried away

DIALOG

A : 왜 동생들한테 고함을 지르니?

Why are you shouting at your brothers?

B : 미안해요. **너무 흥분해서요.**

Sorry. **I got carried away.**

[Note] get carried away는 좋은 뜻으로도 나쁜 뜻으로도 다 사용한다.

584 화면이 희미하다

The picture is blurry.

DIALOG

A : 왜 뒤에 앉기를 좋아하나요?

Why do you prefer the back?

B : 스크린에 너무 가까이 앉으면 **화면이 희미하게 보여서요.**

If we are close to the screen, **the picture will be blurry.**

585 힘들게 만들다

give one a hard time

DIALOG

A : 무엇을 드시겠어요?

What do you want to eat?

B : 전 까다롭지 않아요. 당신 좋아하는 것이면 무엇이나요.

I'm not finicky about food. Whatever you like is okay for me.

A : 나를 **힘들게 하지 말고** 말해 봐요. 뭘 제일 먹고 싶은지.

Please **don't give me a hard time**. Tell me what you would like to eat.

Homecoming

Western News • Fall 1991 • Page 15

Foreign focus

Soon Kwan Kim '81 of South Korea was honored at WIU in July by International Programs for his efforts in recruiting students and providing lodging and hospitality for WIU staff members on their recruiting trips to the Far East. Pictured from left are Assistant to the Dean of Graduate and International Studies Barb Baily, Dean of Graduate and International Studies Suzanne Reid-Williams, Kim, Director of Western English as a Second Language's program Bob Pesek, and Director of International Student Admissions Lu Smith.

웨스턴 일리노이대학 임원들이 서울을 방문할 때마다 도와준 것에 대한 감사패를 받았다.

Courtesy Photo

Soon Kwan Kim, professor of English at Soong Eui Women's Jr. College in Seoul, Korea and a 1981 graduate of Western Illinois University with a master's degree in educational administration, was given a Certificate of Apprciation by Gordon Taylor, director of WIU Alumni Programs at a recent dinner in his honor. Kim was honored for his efforts in recruitment and alumni relations for Western in Korea. Kim has written several books, one of which focuses on American conversation patterns and was edited by several members of the WIU staff.

Thursday, August 1, 1991, The Macomb Journal 5A

웨스턴 일리노이대학 졸업생과 대학과의 관계를 발전시키는 데 기여한 공로로 총동문회장으로부터 감사패를 받았다.

영어회화
요것만 알면!

펴낸날 개정판 1쇄 2018년 9월 9일

지은이 김순관
펴낸이 서용순
펴낸곳 이지출판

출판등록 1997년 9월 10일 제300-2005-156호
주 소 03131 서울시 종로구 율곡로6길 36 월드오피스텔 903호
대표전화 02-743-7661 팩스 02-743-7621
이메일 easy7661@naver.com
디자인 박성현
인 쇄 네오프린텍(주)

값 15,000원

ISBN 979-11-5555-095-3 03740

이 도서의 국립중앙도서관 출판예정도서목록(CIP)은 서지정보유통지원시스템 홈페이지(http://seoji.nl.go.kr)와
국가자료공동목록시스템(http://www.nl.go.kr/kolisnet)에서 이용하실 수 있습니다.(CIP제어번호: CIP2018026972)